The Sporting Scene

White Knights of Reykjavik

By the same author

TOLSTOY OR DOSTOEVSKY

THE DEATH OF TRAGEDY

ANNO DOMINI

LANGUAGE AND SILENCE

IN BLUEBEARD'S CASTLE

EXTRATERRITORIAL

The Sporting Scene

White Knights of Reykjavik

George Steiner

FABER AND FABER
LONDON

First published in The New Yorker 1972
This edition published 1973
by Faber and Faber Limited
3 Queen Square London WC1
Printed and bound
by W & J Mackay Limited, Chatham

ISBN 0 571 10362 6

ACKNOWLEDGEMENTS

This sketch is meant neither for the expert chess player nor the professional historian of the game. Both would find its references to specific games and analytic problems either too elementary or too allusive. I am in no way a qualified analyst of chess and my own game is, by any serious standard, risible. But like countless other *patzers* the world over, I was fascinated by the affair at Reykjavik and by the psychological, political, personal aspects of the Fischer-Spassky match. In this short memoir I have tried to capture something of the bizarre drama of the occasion and something of the autistic passion which lies behind it. I am grateful to Mr. William Shawn, Editor of the *New Yorker*, whose interest made it possible for me to take time off from my normal work in order to go to Iceland. Special thanks are due also to Mr. Walter Goldwater of the Marshall Chess Club in New York who was so kind as to point out a number of errors and misjudgments in the original version of this essay.

G.S.

FACED with Mr. Robert J. Fischer's demand for thirty per cent of the gate receipts of the World Chess Championship Match, in addition to his share of the agreed purse of a hundred and twenty-five thousand dollars and thirty per cent of global film and television rights, an official of the Icelandic Chess Federation remarked desperately, 'This is not Reno'. The differences are indeed unmistakable. For one thing, all bars in Reykjavik are closed on Wednesdays. For another, a blue swastika, the Norse rune for peace and good fortune, is flown over public buildings, in the perennial high winds that always bear the smell of cod. And in July, which was when the match began, there is the light of the unsetting sun. No guide-book quite prepares one for the pressure of the glare from the north as the sun drifts barely below the horizon, keeping the clouds and metallic sea lit through the night hours. There might be a tint of Nevada about the volcanic cones and lava plateau that surround Reykjavik (pop. 82,000), but the texture of rock, ferrous dust, and lichen is utterly different. The edge of ice is never very far off, and the Arctic cold leaves its mildly inebriating taste in the air even on a summer's noon. The long light and rasping winds between stretches of downpour and grey will work on one's nerves. Thus, the lunatic manoeuvres of Bobby Fischer were not the only element to make for jumpiness. Closely confined in a serene but singular life style – the Icelandic language, which is a fairly pure and isolated version of Old Norse, lies like a thorn hedge around those who can neither understand nor speak it – the press corps, estimated at some three hundred reporters, cameramen, addicted literati, and specialists of the game, soon bred its own vacuous fantasies. Reykjavik was, by any practical standards, an odd, taxing venue for the whole affair.

Yet it had its rationale. Though Iceland is a member of NATO and is under the audible shadow of the extensive American Air Force base at Keflavik, it is neutral in tone and forms an almost symbolic halfway house between the United States and the Soviet Union. It is a self-contained land, but jets have made it readily accessible. It is, furthermore, chess-addicted. If the sagas can be trusted, the history of Icelandic chess dates back to about the year 1000. It is detailed in a classic monograph, 'Chess in Iceland', by Professor D. Willard Fiske, of Cornell. Fiske was both a remarkable scholar of early Scandinavian literatures and institutions and a fairly strong player. He was the begetter and secretary of the American Chess Congress of 1857, the first American chess tournament, and was co-editor, with Paul Morphy of one of the earliest American chess magazines, *Chess Monthly*. As far as actual play goes, Fiske's name is still associated with the sixth move P–Q3 in the Two Knights' Defence; he used it against Morphy in a well-known consultation game – three players pooled their wits and knowledge against the master – at the 1857 tournament, in New York. But it is as a historian of chess that he is best remembered, and especially of chess as played in Iceland. Fiske became fascinated by the role of the game in Icelandic myths and society. Printed in Leipzig and written in Icelandic, the chess magazine *I Uppnami* which Fiske published in 1900 and 1901 was among the better chess periodicals in the world at the time. Fiske's *magnum opus* appeared in Florence in 1905, and his collection of chess books can be seen and used in the National Library in Reykjavik.

The 'Heimskringla', a chronicle of the Norse kings, which was probably composed before 1241, refers to King Canute the Great's passion for chess. Snorri Sturluson's saga of St. Olaf tells of a game played on the eve of St. Michael's Day in the year 1027 at the Danish capital of Roskilde. The puissant Jarl, or Earl, Ulf had come to court to regain the King's favour after an act of rebellion. The two men sat down to play. In the course of the game, Canute blundered and left his knight *en prise* (on a square where it could simply be taken). The King asked Ulf to return the piece and allow him a better move. The Earl upset the board and scattered the chessmen on the ground. Fleeing the King's wrath, Ulf sought sanctuary in a church. But the next day the King's men did him to death in the choir. Snorri wrote in *circa* 1230 and may have substituted chess for an older, rather mysterious Norse game called *hnefatafl*, but other thirteenth-century references to Canute's delight in chess make it more than

6

likely that there is truth in the tale, and that chess reached the Norse world, including Iceland, early in the second millennium A.D.

Once it took hold, it flourished. Beginning with the sixteenth century, European visitors commented on the Icelandic passion for the game. In his account of Iceland published in 1561, the Hanseatic merchant and traveller Gories Peerse reported that during the long weeks of winter dark the more prosperous islanders kept to their beds, doing nothing but playing chess, while children and menials tended the house. This, we learn, was particularly the case in Grimsey, a small island within the Arctic Circle, to which Professor Fiske, three hundred years later, donated chess sets and a chess library. In his *Om Iisland*, completed before 1600, the Norwegian priest Peder Clausson Friis mentions marathon games: such are the tenacity and skill of Icelandic players 'that they sometimes spend some weeks' time – playing each day – on a single game, before they can bring it to an end by the victory of the one or the other combatant'. The lust for combat extended to the Church. Stefàn Ólafsson, a priest who lived in the mid-seventeenth century, has left behind a set of imprecations to which any chess addict will respond from the deeps of his black soul:

> My malediction I utter – May Steini's men fall in heaps! May my fearful incantations bewitch him so that peril shall beset two or three of his pieces at once! May the Old One [*gamla*, the queen] lose her life! May the tiny pawns grow fewer and fewer on the squares, and may he be mated with the low and high mates!

Writing in 1694, Sir Robert Molesworth, the English ambassador to the Danish court, wondered at the excellence and prevalence of chess in Iceland. 'It were worth some curious man's enquiry,' he suggested ,'how such a studious and difficult game should get this far northward, and become so generally used.'

The question teases as one looks, in either the British Museum or the National Museum of Antiquities in Edinburgh, at the famous walrus-ivory chessmen found in 1831 in the parish of Uig, on the Hebridean Isle of Lewis. The sea had broken into a subterranean storage room and uncovered these seventy-eight massive, secretive figurines with their worn, regal countenances. In a paper published a year later, the antiquarian and paleographer Sir Frederic Madden assigned these pieces to Iceland. Carved around the year 1200, they had been brought back to the Hebrides across the northern sea as a gift or booty. We do not know for certain, but Madden may well be right. Affinities between the game and the Icelandic setting seem to run deep. Go a few miles out of Reykjavik on roads that soon turn to tracks of flattened lava and the great silences come down – silences that are, as in chess, taut and sometimes menacing. Light and dark divide the Icelandic year between them as they do the board. Ivory is the organic substance most appropriate to the carving of chessmen; it possesses the muted lustre, the tough concavities required by the player's eye and hand. Icelandic history and the ancient fierceness and dignity of the place accord with the game.

These might be fancies. The fact is that the whole of Iceland put unstinted effort and good will into making a success of the World Championship Match between Fischer and Boris Spassky. Numerous countries had expressed interest in staging the event. The United States and Soviet Chess Federations, as well as Fischer personally, rejected most as politically or climatically unacceptable. Spectacular financial bids were entered by Buenos Aires, by Belgrade, and by Reykjavik. After arduous bargaining, it was agreed to hold half the match in Belgrade, starting on 22 June, and half in Iceland. Worried by Fischer's continually mounting exactions and bizarre personal behaviour during the spring, the Yugoslavs asked that a bond be posted insuring his arrival and his readiness to play. Negotiations collapsed in mutual rancour, and Reykjavik found itself saddled with the whole circus. The Icelandic Chess Federation raised an initial two hundred thousand dollars, which happens to be one dollar for every man, woman, and child in the country. Accommodations were found in hotels and private homes – already heavily booked by Iceland's rapidly expanding tourist trade – to provide for an expected inrush of a thousand or more correspondents and chess enthusiasts from all over the world. The

Exhibition Hall in Reykjavik was made ready for twenty-five hundred spectators and a gaggle of five hundred journalists, visiting masters and chess personalities, judges, seconds, and lawyers. In the words of Nikolai Krogius, the most enigmatic but probably also the most influential member of Boris Spassky's entourage, the physical setting provided for the actual games was 'the finest ever devised for an international chess match'. By the start of July – the first game had been scheduled for Sunday, 2 July – Reykjavik was a chess city. Photographs of Spassky and Fischer, chessboards of every size, mockups of giant chessmen, books on the protagonists and their previous games filled shop-windows. At the main crossings in downtown Reykjavik, news vendors were selling first-day covers with fifteen-krona stamps featuring an emblematic rook and a map of the world set out on a chessboard. In the glass and china shops, saltcellars and pepper mills appeared in the guise of queens and bishops. Chess was front- and back-page news in the rival dailies. The Icelandic Chess Federation is, *per capita*, the world's largest, and there can be no doubt that excitement was genuine and pervasive.

With hotel space, airline bookings, telephone lines, the public telegraph office, and every means of local transportation under extreme pressure, with queries and complaints coming at them in every language from Flemish to Japanese, the Icelanders re-mained courteous and endlessly inventive. They found rooms for those who had seen no chess during the first nine days of scheduled play and now clamoured to stay on. They organized sightseeing tours for maddened newsmen. Hammered by Fischer's demands – for quarters more luxurious than the Pres-idential Suite of the Loftleider Hotel, for private use of a swim-ming pool, for a personal tennis court and a Mercedes-Benz with automatic drive, for a cancellation of the television con-tract on which the Icelandic authorities had largely based their budget – Icelandic officials clung almost unfailingly to their good manners and common sense. They gently dismissed Mr. Fischer's outbursts about their 'primitive' country, knowing that it is in fact one of the oldest and most politically sane of Western cul-tures. They offered excuses for his tantrums. Soon one found

9

oneself going around apologizing to the obviously disconcerted but helpful men and women behind the hotel reception desks, behind the shop counters, or in the minute but efficient head-quarters of the Chess Federation. Almost invariably, the response was generous. No one who underwent the long spells of empty waiting and rumour, the opaque press conferences, the hours of general embarrassment and latent hysteria that marked Fischer's late arrival (he lunged out of the plane on 4 July brushing aside the Icelandic notables who had gathered to welcome him), and that debased the early phases of the match, will ever forget the people of Reykjavik or the tone set by Mr. Gudmundur Thorarinsson, the president of the Icelandic Chess Federation, and his colleagues. They had deserved better.

The first 'world-title' tournament was a more disinterested occasion. A number of players of European note met in London in 1851 to find their monarch. First prize and the as yet unofficial world championship went to Adolf Anderssen, a professor of mathematics from Breslau. He was defeated by Paul Morphy, seven wins to two and two games drawn, in a match in Paris played from the twentieth to the twenty-eighth of December, 1858. With Morphy, we move to the distant historical edge of the Fischer world. Parallels between the careers and talents of the two men are suggestive. Born in New Orleans in 1837, Morphy appears to have displayed a real grasp of positional finesse even before he reached the age of twelve. He soon emerged as the top player in a city in which chess was a serious passion. At the celebrated New York tournament in the autumn of 1857, Morphy won fourteen games, lost only one, and drew three. He was now an American legend, and a raid on Europe was inevitable. There ensued a lengthy wrangle with Howard Staunton, the chess columnist of the *Illustrated London News*, the designer of today's standard chess set, and himself among the best English players. The fairest assessment of this acid imbroglio would be that Morphy was justified when he asserted that Staunton was afraid to meet him across the board and that Staunton was using what influence he had to block the triumphant progress of a Yankee intruder. The analogies with some of Fischer's problems and attitudes during the early nineteen-sixties are obvious. Morphy reached England in June, 1858, and proceeded to demolish all comers in a series of individual games, consultation games, simultaneous displays, and games at odds (the opponent usually being given a pawn and a move), which remain among the most dazzling in chess history. Though the rook-and-queen sacrifice that Morphy staged against H. E. Bird was probably unsound – that is to say, subject to theoretical refutation – it remains stunning. So does the tranquil, implacable constriction of Morphy's end play against the Hungarian master J. J. Löwenthal in their game of 21 August. Morphy's descent on Paris was meteoric. One of his spectacular turns was a win over the Duke of Brunswick and Count Isouard de Vauvenargues in the Duke's box at the Opera during the interval in a performance of *The Barber of Seville*. The opposition was not formidable, but time pressed, and Morphy's sacrifice of a knight on the tenth move is as fresh today as it was a little over a century ago.

Having bested Anderssen in a series of games, some of which ran to seven and eight hours, Morphy knew himself to be king. He returned to a triumphal reception in New York in May of 1859. But already he betrayed symptoms of nervous isolation and paranoia. He refused thenceforward to play any American except at odds of a knight. That he continued his string of successes with this handicap is, of course, a further proof of his skill. But he turned fiercely on some of those who had come to do him honour, and took furious exception to any hint, however laudatory, that he was a professional player. Had not his father, Judge Alonzo Morphy, of the High Court of Louisiana, left $146,162.54 at his death, making his son an occasional lawyer and independent gentleman? Back in New Orleans, Morphy challenged any player in the world to meet him at odds of pawn and move. Receiving no answer, he declared his career finished. In fact, he continued to play until 1869, and went to Havana, already a chess centre, to give a blindfold exhibition in February, 1864. But he was increasingly a recluse, and after 1869 his intellect was clouded. The bare mention of chess provoked him to anger. Having conquered all rivals, Morphy disintegrated in a glorious but destructive vacuum. His last years were harrowed by persecution mania. But elements of his relentless style, of his explosive egotism, and of his strategy of general challenge to the world live again in Bobby Fischer. Morphy and Fischer are true compatriots; they play to kill.

Anderssen regained his primacy by winning a tournament in 1862, ahead of Louis Paulsen, a German émigré living in the United States, but he was then defeated in 1866 by the thirty-year-old Wilhelm Steinitz. Steinitz was the first officially acknowledged world champion, and his twenty-eight-year tenure of the crown remains the longest to date. Steinitz, who came from Prague, marks the transition to modern tournament chess. He held off all comers, including players of the calibre of Johannes Zukertort and Mikhail Tchigorin, the originator of many decisive motifs in Russian theory and technique. Unfairly, Steinitz is best remembered for some of the brilliances of which he was the victim toward the end of his great span. Yet one need only look at the fantastic twenty-third and twenty-fourth moves of his game against Kurt von Bardeleben (at Hastings, in England, 1895), when White is under total attack and is threatened with mate but suddenly locates a fatal weakness in Black's king-side position and launches on a ten-move mate of his own, to gauge Steinitz's quality.

His successor is, to my mind, the most attractive of all chess immortals. Dr. Emanuel Lasker, a German, held the title from 1894, when he defeated Steinitz in New York, until 1921, when he was outplayed in Havana by José Raoul Capablanca. Lasker's technique had an unobtrusive universality. A game such as that against W. E. Napier, playing Black, at Cambridge Springs in 1904 remains, to any chess player, at once a wonder and a piece of profound logic. Slight vagaries in Lasker's opening play against a Sicilian Defence gave Napier a chance to initiate a whole set of sparkling combinations. Lasker countered impeccably, but White seemed to have no good continuation after Black's seventeenth move. Then, with an unheralded advance on the wing, Lasker discovered attacking chances. The resulting lines have since been analysed by many commentators. The astounding point is that Lasker and Napier could, to some degree at least, calculate and compare them under stress of actual play. Hard pressed, Napier found a touch of genius on his twenty-first move: N–K5. Though a rook down, he threatened to bring off a mating combination. Under extreme time pressure – each player in modern tournament chess must complete forty moves in two and a half hours – Lasker found the only correct riposte: he returned the rook but won two pawns. The game ended with a chain of White moves, each of which has the hidden transparency of an algebraic solution.

In 1924, no longer world champion, Dr. Lasker came to New York to take part in the International Tournament held that March and April at the Alamac Hotel, on Broadway at Seventy-first Street. This tournament is still, very probably, the strongest in the history of chess. It brought together Capablanca, the world champion, who in the preceding ten years had lost only one game in ninety-five tournament or match trials; the Russian Alexander Alekhine, soon to become world champion; Richard Réti, of Czechoslovakia, whose theories had initiated 'hyper-modern' opening play (openings on the flank and not in the traditional king- or queen-pawn centre); the formidable Savielly Tartakower, from Austria; E. D. Bogolyubov, of the Ukraine, always a dangerous match player; Frank J. Marshall, of the United States; and several other international luminaries. The one hundred and ten games played on this occasion are among the hardest-fought in chess literature, and a good many are among the subtlest. Dr. Lasker won thirteen games outright, twice defeating Réti and Bogolyubov. He drew very difficult games against Alekhine and Capablanca. His only loss was to Capablanca in the fourteenth round, when Lasker, though playing Black, refused a passive, potentially drawing line and went down in a superb end game. A win over Tartakower on 15 April gave Lasker first place and a lasting triumph. He left the hall amid an unstinted ovation.

But Lasker was more than a chess genius. He was very obviously a balanced, widely cultured human being, with interests

13

outside his craft. He was intensity itself during play, but his manners were serenely steady. ('Fischer is almost never still and continually swings around in his special $470 swivel chair while Spassky is deep in thought over his next move. Fischer bites his fingernails, pokes his nose and cleans his ears between moves.' – *International Herald Tribune*, 24 July, 1972.) But then first prize in the 1924 marathon was only fifteen hundred dollars, and the first brilliancy prize, for the single game judged most exciting, only seventy-five dollars – though, report has it, in gold coins.

It is a numbing experience for an ordinary chess player to replay the games of Capablanca. In his study *The Chess Mind*, Gerald Abrahams observes, 'Capablanca possessed a judgment calculated to prevent him from ever risking the loss of control. . . . That, when judgment clashed with judgment, the judgment of Capablanca was almost indefeasible is evidenced by the cold-blooded, and inevitable-seeming, successes of the great master against that considerable virtuoso of aggression, Marshall.' During Capablanca's prime, almost any other name could conclude that sentence. Faced with alternative possibilities, in however intricate or imperilled a position, Capablanca chose the right line. More than any other master, he saw the armature of pure logic, of optimal sequence, which runs like a steel thread beneath the tangle of the board. Capablanca's taut directness is that which chess-playing computers have been programmed for but have, so far, failed to achieve. His brilliancies have a deadly quiet. Both Abrahams and Fred Reinfeld, in his anthology of *Great Brilliancy Prize Games of the Chess Masters*, analyse Capablanca's win over the Austrian Rudolf Spielmann (New York, 1927). White's exchange of a bishop for two pawns on his eighteenth move *is* a dramatic stroke, but when one looks closely it has an almost platitudinous self-evidence. By forcing Black's queen and rook out of position, Capablanca simply clears the terrain for an advance of his own queen to the seventh rank. What follows has the monotony of perfection. An even greater game is the tenth in the 1921 World Championship. It is very difficult to locate any genuine weakness in Lasker's first sixteen moves with White. At this point, controversy and analysis begin. 'The position at Move 17', writes Abrahams, 'may justly be said to be one of the great historic occasions of Chess. Had Lasker avoided loss, the course of Chess history would have been very different.' Whatever the precise cause (did Lasker use the wrong bishop to attack Capablanca's knight?), the champion's queen pawn was weakened. Springing from this one element, the whole of Capablanca's treatment develops with impeccable rigor. Avoiding every trap, every temptation to grasp material advantage prematurely, Capablanca, fifty-one moves later, forced the quietest, most deadly of wins – a pawn advancing to the eighth row to be queened.

Like Fischer, Alexander Alekhine regarded himself as obviously the greatest player in the world. 'I dominate them all!' Many would argue that were he alive today his pre-eminence would still be manifest. He was born in Moscow in 1892 and emigrated to Paris after the Revolution, becoming a French citizen. Nevertheless, Alekhine's career may be said to mark the beginning of the Russian edge in world chess. The point is worth making, because one often gets the impression that Russian players have been overlords throughout modern chess. This is not so. During the nineteenth century, to be sure, the Russians Carl Jaenisch, Alexander Petrov, and Tchigorin were masters of world class. Alekhine himself grew up under the influence and challenge of Akiba Rubinstein. But it was not until his own performance and, in fact, not until the late 1940s that Russian players and the Russian school of chess became overwhelming in international encounters. Alekhine was a bitter opponent of the Soviet regime and ended his career as a muddled pro-Nazi. Frequently his public conduct verged on the pathological. Sad, sordid episodes accompanied his declining years. His games, in contrast, have an unsurpassed beauty. 'He is a poet', writes Dr. Max Euwe, of the Netherlands, who was to defeat Alekhine for the world title in 1935, and whose presiding role in Reykjavik during the first days of July provided a moving link with the great past: 'He is a poet, who creates a work of art out of something which would hardly inspire another man to send home a picture postcard. The wilder and more involved a position, the more beautiful the conception he can evolve.' Almost helpless against Capablanca in his early years of play (witness his catastrophic defeat in the 1914 St. Petersburg Tournament), Alekhine overcame the Cuban giant in an exhausting match in Buenos Aires in 1927. He regained his crown from Euwe in 1937 and held it until his death in 1946. Such was the inventive shapeliness of Alekhine's strategy that it made some of his opponents into much greater artists than they ordinarily were. It may be that Alekhine smashed every bit of furniture in his Carlsbad hotel room in 1923 after losing a King's Indian Defence to F. D. Yates, of Great Britain. But, as Reinfeld puts it, the game itself is 'the most beautiful ever won from the most brilliant player of all time'. Paradoxical as this may sound, only Alekhine could have set the deep trap which Yates entered and from which he emerged to win.

In Moscow during a simultaneous display in 1925, Capablanca, the world champion, resigned on the thirty-second move of a Queen's Gambit to a fourteen-year-old Leningrad schoolboy, Mikhail Botvinnik. During the important tournament staged at Nottingham in August of 1936, Alekhine seemed to have a clear win against Botvinnik when the latter found an exceedingly subtle line with which to force a draw. When they met again in Holland two years later, Botvinnik, with White, beat Alekhine in a game that remains a classic of positional logic. Botvinnik is unquestionably a player of great power; his technique in the end game comes near to perfection. But his triumph over four other contenders at the world-title tournament organized at The Hague in 1948 by the International Chess Federation (FIDE) represents a more general change in the structure and climate of master chess. Behind Botvinnik's ten wins, two losses, and eight draws lay the collaborative discipline and collective analysis that had boosted Soviet chess to a new level of theoretical and psychological preparation. Botvinnik summarizes the story in his well-known article on 'The Russian and Soviet School of Chess'. No society, no political system had ever invested comparable energies in the perfection of a pastime. From earliest childhood

on, a Soviet chess player benefited from a degree of formal training, of scrutiny by his seniors, of public notice, of material support and potential acclaim that no other country could hope to
equal. An entire edifice of national values and didactic aims,
with which even Stalin seems to have been involved, underlies
a characteristic news item for 1935: 'S. Orjonikidze, the People's
Commissar of Heavy Industry, issued a special order noting the
achievements of Mikhail Botvinnik, graduate student at the
Leningrad Industrial Institute, in combining serious research
work in electrical engineering with star chess performance.' By
1952, the grandmaster had twice been decorated with the Order
of the Badge of Honour. The second commendation cites not
only Botvinnik's excellence as a player but his ability, characteristic of Soviet man, to 'take a clear, objective view of his short-
comings, even the slightest ones, and work persistently to root
them out'.

Botvinnik's first two defences of his world title, against David
Bronstein in 1951 and against Vasily Smyslov in 1954, illustrate
the extreme strength of Soviet chess. Both ended in draws, in
which event the incumbent retains the title. In 1957, Smyslov
beat Botvinnik. A year later, Botvinnik regained his title. The
world championship had now become a Russian carrousel.
Players such as Yefim Geller, Paul Keres, Vyacheslav Ragozin,
Mark Taimanov, Alexander Tolush, Victor Korchnoi, and Igor
Bondarevsky were often only points apart on a ladder to which
no outsider seemed to have access. At the Candidates' Tournament held in Switzerland in 1953, only one foreign contestant,
Miguel Najdorf, of Argentina, could break even against Soviet
players. This domination was to last at least until 1970, at which
point the Russian side just squeaked home against the Rest of the
World team but lost over the first nine boards. (Had Keres not
won beautifully on the bottom board, the Soviet era would have
been formally closed.)

A new star emerged from this bright cluster. The U.S.S.R.
Championship of 1957 was won by a twenty-year-old student in
the Department of History and Philology of Riga University,
Mikhail Tal. Three years later, Tal wrested the world title from

Botvinnik in a fascinating match in Moscow (six wins, two defeats, thirteen draws). Tal is a player of phenomenal invention and sparkle, one of the great 'naturals' in chess. Though in 1961 Botvinnik once more recaptured his crown, there was every prospect of a Tal era. Tal's health, however, proved unable to sustain the tearing physical and mental pressures of match play at the top. He continues to produce flashing games but has to a large extent dropped out of the international circuit. Tal's absence has a bearing on Fischer's ascent. Already at the end of the 1950s, competent observers were hoping for and predicting a world-title duel between these two immensely gifted young masters. Whenever they did meet, the results were exhilarating. Playing Black and a Sicilian, Tal convincingly routed Fischer at the Candidates' Tournament in Yugoslavia in 1959; Fischer avenged his loss two years later at Bled. Both games are a joy, although – or because – they fully illustrate Fischer's maxim 'In top-flight chess, you have to drive your advantage home unmercifully'. The last time they fought, at Curaçao on 5 June, 1962, Fischer and Tal drew after the most classical, mutually respectful of games (a Ruy Lopez). Tal's potential against Fischer may remain one of the sad unknowns in modern chess.

Tal's eclipse opened the way to a player who is in every respect his opposite. Born in Tiflis in 1929, Tigran Petrosian became U.S.S.R. Junior Champion at the age of seventeen with a staggering fourteen out of a possible fifteen points. He earned the rank of grandmaster in 1952 after tying for second place with Taimanov at the Interzonal Tournament in Stockholm. He defeated Botvinnik in Moscow in 1963 to take the world championship. Of eminent masters, Petrosian is the most boring. His finest games are draws. When Fischer finally managed a win over Petrosian, it was after the Armenian had offered a draw and had blundered, probably out of vexation, when Fischer declined. (Fischer's annotation at this point in *My 60 Memorable Games* is illuminating: 'I was ready to accept, but Tal happened to be standing there at that instant, hovering anxiously, since a drawn result would practically clinch first place for him. So I refused – not because I thought White had anything in the position, but because I didn't want to give Tal the satisfaction!') Petrosian's draws are, however, rather special. He plays a brand of chess that is at once passive and wily. Often, he will bring back a piece to its starting position in what appear to be empty manoeuvres. Yet at his best he will spin a tough, ultimately fatal net out of some seemingly inert detail of control or configuration. Carried away by the static subtlety of this method, a number of Petrosian's opponents have declared him to be 'the hardest player in history to defeat'.

This, certainly, was Spassky's experience when he challenged the champion for world mastery in Moscow in 1966. Having overcome Keres (perhaps the finest chess player never to be champion), Geller, and the ailing Tal, Spassky entered the contest a firm favourite. His style was expected to tell early and decisively. The first six games were drawn. During the seventh game, Spassky's patience faltered, and Petrosian ground ahead to win with Black. The tenth game was a handsome victory for the champion. The thirteenth, a ninety-one-move monster that left both players exhausted, gave Spassky his first win. But Petrosian continued to play exasperatingly complex defensive chess, and the challenger could only equalize in the nineteenth game. By that point, his resources were spent, and Petrosian went on to retain his title by a one-game margin.

Spassky's second crack at the world crown came in 1969. He eliminated Geller, Korchnoi, and Bent Larsen, of Denmark, in a series of matches which include the finest attacking chess of his career. Spassky's seventh game against Korchnoi, when he broke through a King's Indian Defence and clinched the game with a queen sacrifice, is one of the classics in modern chess. The challenger trained intensively for the Petrosian match, with a cross-country run each morning and a daily session of yoga. Nikolai Krogius and Igor Bondarevsky, both of whom are themselves grandmasters, guided Spassky in his strategic and psychological preparations. Spassky lost the first game, most likely owing to an attack of nerves (this is a curious, repeated pattern in world championships). But after that he pulled steadily ahead. The crisis came in Games Nine to Seventeen.

Having missed a winning line in the ninth game, Spassky seemed to go groggy. Petrosian equalized the score and embarked on a row of characteristic draws. He had reason to believe that Spassky was now worn out and the 1966 scenario would be repeated. But this time his adversary got a formidable second wind. His victory in the nineteenth game had dramatic authority, leaving Petrosian's king side a shambles. Petrosian's comeback in Game Twenty was his last. Spassky won Game Twenty-one, and two further draws gave him the magic twelve and a half points he needed. Before a wildly enthusiastic audience in Moscow, Dr. Euwe, the president of FIDE, presented the new world champion with his gold medal.

The road had not been an easy one. Boris Spassky, who, like Fischer, is a second child and who is also of Jewish descent (on the maternal side), was born in Leningrad in January, 1937. He was evacuated to Moscow soon after war broke out and did not return until 1946, when the partly destroyed city was still in the grip of hunger. Spassky's parents were divorced in 1944. Again the parallel with Fischer is interesting: both were brought up by strong mothers, and experienced solitude, displacement, and material anxieties in their early childhood. Spassky learned the rudiments of chess at the age of five but did not receive any systematic instruction until he joined the chess club of the Leningrad Palace of Young Pioneers, in the autumn of 1946. His first trainer was Vladimir Zak, whose favourite version of the Nimzo-Indian Defence became one of Spassky's hallmarks. In 1947, when Spassky was all of ten, he won a 'best game' prize for one of his games in the Junior Championship of the Russian Chess Federation. He became Junior Champion of Leningrad only two years later. From then on, the attention of the Soviet chess hierarchy was focused on his progress. 'Between 1946 and 1950,' recalls Spassky, 'I regularly played up to five hours a day.' From 1952 onward, Botvinnik took a watchful interest in the development of the young master. Spassky was a member of the Soviet side in the strong International Tournament in Bucharest in 1953, and beat Smyslov with precisely the opening variation

Zak had taught him (B–N5 on the fourth move). He was now sixteen and, like Bobby Fischer, found school irksome. 'Fischer is completely right,' comments Spassky, 'when he says that it is a bad idea for a chess master to study hard at school or college.' He excelled in athletics, majored in journalism, a soft option, and concentrated on his true métier.

After his Bucharest showing, Spassky was awarded the title of international master by FIDE. (Successive gradations of master, international master, and international grandmaster, or simply grandmaster, a title held at last count by ninety-eight men, are awarded by the Federation according to an intricate system of points won in tournaments of increasing strength and representation.) The year 1955 was a highlight. Spassky came equal with Petrosian and Botvinnik and was only half a point behind the joint victors Smyslov and Geller in the Twenty-second U.S.S.R. Championship. In his games against grand-masters, he had scored five points out of eight. As the British master Leonard Barden puts it in his informative foreword to *Spassky's 100 Best Games*, the young star had emerged as 'the crown prince of world chess'. He had become the youngest player ever to qualify for the Interzonal – one of the crucial steps to the final challenge. In 1955, at a tournament in Antwerp, Spassky became Junior World Champion with a blitzing record of eight out of nine. He was now the youngest grandmaster in the history of the game. In the 1956 Candidates' Tournament, Spassky finished third, with only Smyslov and Keres, players of vastly superior experience, in front of him. Already he was being referred to as the next Capablanca.

Instead, there ensued a period of crisis and acute setbacks, lasting from late 1956 to almost the end of 1961. Spassky seemed to have lost his grip both on chess and on his personal life. Tal easily outdistanced him in the U.S.S.R. Championship of 1957 and worsted him again at the Zonal Tournament for the world-title challenge held in Riga in 1958. 'When I resigned,' reports Spassky, 'there was a thunder of applause but I was in a daze and hardly understood what was happening. I was certain the world went down; I felt there was something terribly wrong.

After this game I went on the street and cried like a child.' A comparable disaster occurred three years later. Spassky resigned a vital game against the Russian grandmaster Leonid Stein, only to discover, too late, that Stein's intended continuation after the adjournment would have been a crass blunder. The warmth of encouragement offered a Soviet master by his peers and by the authorities is matched by their virulence and publicity of reproof. Having lost at top board in the World Students' Team Championship in Leningrad in 1960 against the Reverend William Lombardy, of the United States (Father Lombardy was Fischer's second in Reykjavik), Spassky underwent harsh official criticism. He was accused of lack of thoroughness in his training for match play and was dropped from the Soviet team in a number of foreign tournaments. Spassky and his wife were divorced in 1961; according to Spassky, they had become 'like bishops of opposite colours'. He also broke with his trainer, Tolush. He went over to Bondarevsky, and began regaining confidence. When one looks back, however, this change takes on an ambiguous significance. Tolush is a player of utmost aggressiveness and risk. His win over Victor Ciociltea, of Rumania (Bucharest, 1953), is among the more ferocious onslaughts in the literature of king-side attacks. Had Spassky continued to train with Tolush, Fischer's style might have carried less menace.

Nevertheless, these deep changes in Spassky's private and professional life, together with a brilliant performance at Mar del Plata, in Argentina, in the spring of 1960, in which he routed Fischer with a King's Gambit, did mark the turn of the tide. Spassky played solidly at Baku in late 1961 to capture the U.S.S.R. Championship. The decisive breakthrough came three years later, during the 1964 Interzonal in Amsterdam. Spassky still thinks of this tournament as the most taxing in his career. He tied for first place with Smyslov, Tal, and Larsen. After eight years of ups and downs, he was again a crown prince. His style had gained immeasurably in edge and assurance: his winning combinations against Alberto Foguelman, Georgi Tringov, and Pal Benko (always a giant-killer) show an entirely new degree of incisiveness. Even more significantly, Spassky had begun to display a certain savagery. He knew of Tal's unstable health and at the 1965 Candidates' Tournament he planned accordingly: 'Draw, draw, and draw again, reserving my final kick for the end of the match when I was gaining in strength and Tal was becoming weaker.' Spassky's win over Tal's Ruy Lopez in the eleventh game remains a model of patience and calculated counter-stroke. Only a truly great player would have removed his queen from a severely threatened king side, as Spassky did on his twenty-sixth move, thus initiating and ultimately insuring decisive simplifications in the centre of the board.

Though he was, as we have seen, repulsed by Petrosian in his 1966 challenge, Spassky hardly broke stride. In the same year, he came ahead of both Petrosian and Fischer at Santa Monica. His second marriage, in 1967, obviously strengthened his confidence. In 1968, he defeated Larsen crushingly both in their Candidates' Match and at the Lugano Olympiad. There was no reason to suppose that Spassky would not be a worthy champion. Having gained the title, in 1969, he spoke of playing a hundred tournament games a year and of putting his reputation on the line even at the risk of losing to weaker opponents. Events turned out rather differently. Spassky began playing less, and cautiously. He was content to register draws (ten out of twelve games at Leiden in 1970). Contestants such as Vlastimil Hort, of Czechoslovakia, and Hans Ree, of the Netherlands, either came in front of Spassky or tied with him at a number of minor international venues. Only two games of real importance marked the reign of the new king. Spassky pounded Larsen in the U.S.S.R. vs. Rest of the World mêlée, in a game whose closing offer of a pawn and sacrifice of a knight and a rook defies belief. And he beat Fischer at the Siegen Olympiad. The game itself, a Grünfeld Defence, is of no great quality, but Spassky's unrelenting pressure did expose odd weaknesses in Fischer's repertoire. At the end of 1971, Spassky came a poor sixth at the Alekhine Memorial Tournament, in Moscow. There was a wistful touch to his remark 'I'm still king, you know'. But had he not defeated Fischer or drawn with him in all their five encounters?

To meet Boris Spassky is a privilege. (On the morning of 14 July, during breakfast at the Saga Hotel, I was, by mere chance, the one to take him a six-page screed in which Fischer explained his refusal to play the night before and threatened to break off the whole match. The courtly sadness of Spassky's remark to me – 'This letter is about everything except chess' – was characteristic.) He is an invididual of great charm and impeccable courtesy. In contrast to Fischer, Spassky's literacy is wide and his political awareness is at once subtle and adult. He is steeped in Dostoevski and Solzhenitsyn. He has never joined the Party. When Czech players wore black armbands at an international tournament shortly after the Soviet invasion of August, 1968, Spassky was the only Russian to venture a gesture of discreet sympathy, which was to shake each of them by the hand. There are, in short, sources of profound private strength and conviction in his often relaxed and humorous personality. He is a prodigiously talented, well-rounded master of the game. He would not otherwise have been world champion in the era of Keres, Tal, Bronstein, Larsen, and Fischer. But his humane distinction has made for certain key weaknesses. Spassky is prone to bouts of melancholy, of introspective passivity (the Oblomovism of Russian literature and life). In the final analysis, qualities of consciousness – of perception – seem to matter more to him than does chess. He lacks the killer's bite, the monomaniacal tension that compels victory out of some minute positional advantage and that seeks to smash the very core of an opponent. Spassky's calm at the chessboard, even when he is in bad trouble, is famous. In part, it results from the good manners of a gentleman and from the self-control of a great technician. But it may also reflect an ultimate dispassion toward the game – a realization, perhaps subconscious, that it is not, as Fischer proclaims, 'everything'. Boris Spassky's fineness as a man and vulnerability as a player were to count heavily during the long summer of 1972.

By now, Fischer's life is legend. Joe Glazer and his Fianchettoed Bishops have twanged 'The Ballad of Bobby Fischer' across the land. Fischer's slack but at moments lupine features have glanced absently at a dazzled world from the covers of *Life*, the *Times Magazine, Newsweek, Time, Der Spiegel*, and a dozen other international weeklies. Frank Brady published a first biography of Fischer, *Profile of a Prodigy*, in 1965 and is currently at work on a second. Fischer has received an epistle of support from President Nixon and an anxious call from Dr. Kissinger (at the time when it seemed he would refuse to play out the match). David Frost has wafted Fischer's six-foot-two frame to Bermuda for lunch. Harold Schonberg, senior music critic of the *Times*, has invited him to a Rubinstein concert and has reported the fact in *Harper's*. Is there any innocent left, from San Francisco to Vladivostok, who has not heard of 'Bobby the inscrutable. Bobby the *enfant terrible*. Bobby the monomaniac. Bobby the recluse. Bobby the international grandmaster. Bobby the Mozart of chess' (Mr. Schonberg again)? By dint of his compelling presence and public strategies, Fischer has modified the social, professional aspects of a game that is perhaps fifteen hundred years old. He has made world headlines and popular features of a totally abstract, esoteric, terribly narrow cerebral hobby. He has boosted ten- and twentyfold the financial rewards at the summit. (His final benefits from the Icelandic match may exceed two hundred thousand dollars; the top purse ever put up in a previous chess match was twelve thousand, but most great tournaments netted the winner one thousand or twenty-five hundred.) He has generated a chess fever across the United States, which previously counted only thirty-seven thousand players who had bothered to register with the United States Chess Federation. These are staggering achievements for a twenty-nine-year-old loner whose bad manners and indifference to customary social behaviour and to the personal feelings of others verge on the transcendent. They point to a somnambular certainty of touch and to a peculiar force of the kind marshalled by great or predatory political figures and, in exceptional instances, by performing artists of genius. Such explosive world fame and the eerie splendour of Fischer's play since his demolition of Petrosian in five hours and thirty-nine moves in Belgrade on the afternoon of 29 March, 1970, have given an impression of unbroken, meteoric pre-eminence. The facts are more complicated. In certain regards, Fischer's ups and downs have been scarcely less drastic than Spassky's.

In an essay the American grandmaster Arthur Bisguier contributes to the compendium *The Games of Robert J. Fischer*, he compares Fischer to another American star, Samuel Reshevsky and remarks, 'Although certainly gifted, Fischer was not a prodigy in the sense that Reshevsky was a prodigy. Reshevsky was playing strong and winning chess from the time he was six, and though Bobby knew the moves at this age and later was involved in tournaments at the Y.M.C.A. and Brooklyn Chess Club, it was not until the middle 1950s that he succeeded in winning any event.' The difference is this: by his fifteenth year Fischer had played several individual games that contained genuinely creative ideas and one game, at least, that ranks among the 'Evergreens' of chess. His fortieth move against Attilio di Camillo in the 1956 Eastern States Open, forcing instant victory, is one that Alekhine would have been proud of. (Fischer was thirteen.) His find of Q–K2 ch on the seventh move against William Addison's Caro-Kann Defence in the U.S. Open of 1957 is a powerful addition to our sense of White's possibilities. So is his advance of a bishop pawn on move fourteen of his game against Arthur Feuerstein in the 1957–58 United States Championship. The most famous game of Fischer's youth, perhaps of his career so far, is, of course, that against Donald Byrne in the Lessing J. Rosenwald Tournament of 1956. In that tournament, the young master registered a negative score, but the seventeenth move of his Grünfeld Defence against Byrne may well, as Brady asserts, 'be talked about for centuries to come', and it assuredly 'established his place among the great chess prodigies of all time'. Moving his queen bishop to K3, Fischer deliberately sacrificed his queen (or, more exactly and relevantly, he forced Byrne to capture). This sacrifice leads to a win in *all* conceivable variations. Only a thorough chess player will be able to picture at all clearly the depth, the imaginative grasp, the sheer reach of calculation involved in Fischer's manoeuvre. The mate comes twenty-four moves later but is already dynamically, inexorably latent in Fischer's quiet stroke. To be crowned champion of the United States, a full point ahead of Reshevsky, and after a tournament in which he went undefeated, was an utterly fantastic result for a boy not yet fifteen. But it counted less than the fact that he had entered the history of the game itself by his originality and theoretic penetration. In this respect, the early Fischer stands beside Capablanca.

A year later, the champion dropped out of school, which he found a contemptible waste of his time, and began life as a free-lance. His first important international foray came at Portoroz, Yugoslavia, in 1958. He managed draws with both Tal and Petrosian. Af fifteen, Fischer was an international grandmaster, qualified to compete for the right to challenge the world champion. At the 1959 Candidates' Tournament, he tied for fifth and sixth place. Though he had lost all his games against Tal and beaten Petrosian only once, he had scored remarkable wins over Smyslov and Keres. The fact that Keres, for all his experience and stature, blundered hopelessly on his twenty-fourth move shows something of the psychological pressure Fischer already exercised. Yet Fischer was acutely disappointed. He had come to Yugoslavia fully intent on being the youngest challenger ever, perhaps even the youngest victor, in a world-title trial. From this disappointment date the first of the acrid professional and private quarrels that have shadowed the whole of his career. His eminence as a player, however, seemed to be rocketing. At Mar del Plata, Fischer tied with Spassky for first and second place with an overwhelming total of thirteen and a half points out of a possible fifteen. Then, abruptly, occurred the worst débâcle of his international record: three months later, at the Buenos Aires Sesquicentennial Tournament, Fischer ranked thirteenth, with a minus score. The lighting, he declared, had been intolerable. Somehow, the lamps had shone differently on Reshevsky and Korchnoi. Chastened and angry, Fischer led a formidable United States team to the Olympiad in Leipzig. Twenty-four grandmasters, thirty-seven international masters, and a hundred and twenty-three masters, representing forty nations, had assembled for the event. Fischer played beautifully, drawing with Tal and losing only to Svetozar Gligorić, the inspired Yugoslav grandmaster, who was to become one of his few firm friends. Brady justly cites a closing rook-and-queen combination in a victory over Martner Letelier, of Chile, as one of the most nearly perfect in Fischer's record. On the final ladder, the United States came a brilliant second to the Soviet Union.

In July and August, 1961, the American Chess Foundation, with the help of private patrons, sponsored a sixteen-game match between Reshevsky and Fischer, which ended in a spectacular row. Personal bitterness of a stridency rare even in the antagonistic ambience of master chess had divided the two men almost from the moment of their first meeting. Everything in Reshevsky's ponderous style and somewhat censorious manner infuriated the hungry Fischer. Neither would make the slightest concession to the other's habits or wishes. With the score at five and a half points each, Fischer broke off. The legal merits of his behaviour (the exact point at issue being whether or not he had been consulted about the scheduling of a game) have been argued to this day. They are a trivial bore. The pity is that the dispute almost entirely obscured the quality of the games. Reshevsky's victories in the first and seventh are among the best in the magisterial career of the old fox. Fischer's comeback against the Dragon Variation of the Sicilian in Game Two is a thing of beauty. I would guess that this tense, personally wretched mêleé was in fact one of the crucial episodes in Fischer's seasoning. In the immediate context, however, matters were not improved by a manic and generally insulting interview Fischer gave to Ralph Ginzburg, for *Harper's*. When it appeared, in January, 1962, Reshevsky's case seemed to have been made for him.

Meanwhile, however, Fischer's progress as a tournament giant was unimpeded. In an extremely strong field at Bled, Fischer won against Tal (at last!) and against Petrosian and Geller. He spun a delicate mating web around the ever-wary Petrosian. He crushed Geller, one of the most resistant players alive, in only twenty-two moves. He emerged from the tournament undefeated. Even Reshevsky was aroused to approving comment. The Interzonal in Stockholm followed quickly at the start of 1962. Fischer's performance was nothing short of majestic. He won the event two and one half points ahead of Geller and Petrosian. A month before his nineteenth birthday, he stood poised very close to the pinnacle of world chess. He had shown a technical flair, an inexorability (for example, in a win over Korchnoi) fully comparable with that of a Capablanca. Readers' polls taken by Soviet chess publications placed the American star just below Tal at the top of the world roster. Now there were eight aspirants left before the final hurdle, the Candidates' Tournament to be played in Curaçao, in the Netherlands Antilles, during the spring of 1962. Excitement about Fischer's achievements in Bled and Stockholm had fired the chess world. As Keres noted, 'the young American grandmaster is absolutely the No. 1 favourite'.

The catastrophe at Curaçao has often been recounted. Fischer managed to win as many games as any other candidate, but he lost seven. He finished fourth, three full points after the leaders, Petrosian, Geller, and Keres. (Ill health had forced Tal out of the tournament.) There have been interminable post mortems. Pal Benko, who trounced Fischer at the very start, said that there was no mystery: Fischer simply wasn't the best player there. But after the great run of masterpieces in Yugoslavia and Sweden, Fischer's poor showing at the board and the irascible eccentricity of his personal conduct during the whole tournament do pose a problem. It may be that he was in some measure exhausted after the Reshevsky tussle and the strain of two fierce international occasions. At a deeper level, Curaçao may have brought into the open a dramatic lack of balance between a chess virtuoso and a human being who had come of age with hardly the rudiments of an education, with hardly the first notions of ordinary human contact and emotional maturity. There was now an almost pathological one-sidedness to Fischer's outlook and personality. He was a young man of nineteen with the chess brain of a complete master and the emotional, intellectual reserves in all other regards of a raw adolescent.

When the explosion came, it proved destructive. In a notorious manifesto published in *Sports Illustrated* for 20 August,

29

1962, Fischer declared that 'the Russians have fixed world chess'. Animated by the evils of Communism, by chauvinistic frenzy, and by their obvious panic at Fischer's genius, Soviet masters had pre-plotted their games with one another so as to insure swift, restful draws. This spared them exhausting end games and adjournments, and enabled them to spend quiet hours in consultation against Fischer. When they played *him*, each game was prolonged to its merciless conclusion and was conducted with the benefit of massive collaborative advice from the whole Soviet pack. FIDE, moreover, was a mere stooge of Soviet chess imperialism. The whole pyramid of Interzonals and Candidates' Tournaments was calculated to insure that 'there will always be a Russian world champion'. The John Birch Society, with some of whose adherents Fischer may have begun to have contacts at about this time, was right: in chess, as in all other international activities, Moscow was out to cheat and enslave the free world. Fischer would no longer be taken for a ride. He would participate in no tournaments organized by FIDE. He would remain content with being 'champion of the Free World'. Anyone but a *patzer* or a Commie knew who was No. 1 anyway.

In the nature of the case, it is difficult either to prove or to disprove Fischer's charge regarding 'grandmaster draws' between Soviet contenders. Benko, a Hungarian refugee with no love for the Russians, denied it flatly. Keres maintained, somewhat questionably, that draws could only benefit those in the lower half of the table. Leonard Barden and some on-the-spot observers were less certain. FIDE itself, however stringent its denials at the time, did take steps to meet Fischer's points. Though the interzonal mechanism remains, the candidates' elimination was simplified so that the loser of each match would be knocked out *vis-à-vis* a given rival, instead of having to continue in a tiring round robin. Judges were urged to enforce the rule that a draw in under thirty moves is not permitted. (As it happened, Fischer was one of the first to violate it, but he explained, 'Those rules are for Communist cheaters, not for me'.) Nonetheless, whatever the merits of his indictment, Fischer's career as an international luminary and probable world champion seemed to lie in ruins. His moody aggressiveness in Curaçao – where he had pronounced the food, the playing conditions, and the behaviour of other players to be quite intolerable – had confirmed the worst that had been said about his character. After Curaçao began the most unstable, apparently self-destructive years of his life.

To be sure, Fischer continued to produce some glorious chess. His massacre of the field at the United States Championship in December, 1963, and January, 1964, was so definitive that he has scarcely felt the urge since to demonstrate his total primacy over American competition. Though only a miniature of twenty-one moves, Fischer's successful Grünfeld Defence against Robert Byrne (the brother of Donald) produced what many connoisseurs regard as one of the deepest, most complicated conceptions in the history of master play. His King's Gambit against Larry Evans in the same tournament is sheer magic. And even though Fischer's $5\frac{1}{2}$–$5\frac{1}{2}$ score at the Olympiad in Varna, on the Black Sea, was a severe comedown, his twenty-four-move demolition of Najdorf, an immensely experienced, resourceful opponent, was the high point of the occasion. But at Varna Fischer also betrayed how deeply he had become enmeshed in the cocoon of his resentments. Using a variation first worked out by Smyslov, Fischer outplayed the world champion, Botvinnik, in the opening stages of a Grünfeld. By the thirty-second move, he had a real advantage. The game was adjourned on the forty-fifth. Analysing all night (a perfectly legitimate practice), Botvinnik and Geller found subtle possibilities of counter-attack. The next day, on the sixty-eighth move, this tremendous duel was drawn. Fischer was incensed. Had he not announced beforehand that he could give Botvinnik odds and beat him? He demanded that an official complaint be lodged, on the absurd ground that the Russian team captain, Lev Abramov, had whispered to and smiled at Botvinnik, obviously giving him vital aid. Once again, proclaimed Fischer, 'Commie cheaters' had robbed him of his just reward.

After Varna, Fischer did play from time to time in international chess – notably at the Havana Olympiad in 1966, at

Skoplje in 1967, and at Natanya, in Israel, in 1968, whee her came first and brought off a fine win against Ciociltea. But he was making things ever more difficult for himself and the rest of mankind. Having joined the Church of God, a fundamentalist Christian Sabbatarian sect based in California, Fischer would no longer play or allow any worldly intrusion between sundown on Friday and sundown on Saturday. (Was this, I wonder, a delayed riposte to Reshevsky's Orthodox Judaism and *its* Sabbath adjournments?) When he was invited to play abroad for the United States or in domestic tournaments, often staged in the express hope of luring the sulking Achilles from his tent, he demanded fees that seemed either scandalous or simply unobtainable. (Already, Reykjavik has turned this very recent past in the economics of chess into prehistory.) He stalked out of the Interzonal in Sousse in October, 1967, after an acrimonious dispute over playing conditions and schedule – but also when leading and after a memorable draw with Korchnoi and a quick 'crusher' over Byrne. By 1970, few would have dissented from the judgment of Hans Kmoch, a veteran player and commentator on the game: 'Finally the U.S.A. produces its greatest chess genius and he turns out to be just a stubborn boy.'

To everyone's surprise, Fischer agreed to play in the U.S.S.R. vs. Rest of the World challenge at Belgrade in March, 1970. (Even during his years of eclipse, Fischer was idolized in Yugoslavia.) Surprise spiralled to sheer disbelief when he consented to play second board behind Larsen, whose international record had during the past year been more active and scintillating than his own. Fischer entered the hall, glanced momentarily at Larsen and Spassky on No. 1, and quietly sat down to face Petrosian. What followed makes for one of the most remarkable pages in the history of chess.

As I have already mentioned, Fischer won a superb opening game. On 31 March, playing Black in an English Opening, he won again. He drew the third and fourth in the set. This showing was not only formidable in itself. It restored Fischer's self-confidence and released unprecedented psychological and technical energies in his game. Only weeks later, he won the Tournament of Peace in Rovinj and Zagreb, drawing with Smyslov and beating Gligorić and the very fine East German master Wolfgang Uhlmann. In December, he swept the Interzonal in Palma de Mallorca with fifteen wins, seven draws, and only one loss – to Larsen. Psychologically, Fischer's authoritative win over Geller in a seventy-two-move classic and his demolition of Taimanov's Sicilian on 6 and 7 December must have been of the first importance. Almost overnight, the chance to play for, and to seize, the world crown was again within his grasp. Fischer's defeat of Reshevsky at this tournament, with a cruel stab at White's seventh rank, was little more than a tigerish afterthought. The past no longer counted.

Fischer played the first of his Candidates' Matches against Taimanov in May and June, 1971. As far back as 1958, the Soviet chess hierarchy had criticized their young master (who is also an accomplished musician) for 'his underestimation of the strength of his opponents'. Nevertheless, Taimanov's international performance had often proved dangerous, and he came to Vancouver for the match with a by no means negligible record. He showed real strength in the first game, but weakened in a difficult conclusion; he blundered away a draw in the second; he missed what was arguably a winning line in the third; he lost to a fierce Fischer onslaught in the fourth; he had a draw in the fifth but threw away a rook; he was hardly a presence in the sixth, and last. There had not been so one-sided a score at this level of chess since Steinitz hammered Joseph Blackburne, of England, by seven games to nil in 1876. In July, Fischer descended on Denver to play Bent Larsen. At the time, Larsen was the finest player, besides Fischer, in the West. He had won matches against Geller and Tal. He had brought off victories against Fischer on earlier occasions. He was famous for his strategic grasp and combativeness. But at once he was in fearful trouble. In a memorable first game, Fischer assumed complete tactical sovereignty. In the second game, Larsen blundered away two vital pawns. Fischer brushed aside his Sicilian Defence in Game Three. Desperate to get back into the match, Larsen developed what seemed a very strong position against Fischer's King's

Indian in the fourth game, only to make inconsistent, ultimately losing choices on his twenty-third and twenty-seventh moves. He could have obtained solid equality in the fifth game but went in for a complicated risky line and lost. He disdained the chance of a consolation draw through perpetual check on the last day of the match and went down to annihilation. On 30 September, 1971, in Buenos Aires, Fischer sat down to play Petrosian. The latter had just eliminated Korchnoi by winning a ninth game after eight consecutive draws. Excitement in the San Martín Theatre was at fever pitch and spilled over into crowds massed in the streets outside. Repeatedly, the U.S.S.R. Championship, then being held in Leningrad, was interrupted as players examined the moves relayed from Argentina. Fischer took Game One, though in bad time trouble. But on 5 October the miraculous streak ended; Fischer handled his Grünfeld Defence rather casually and was crushed. Three draws followed. Petrosian's feline precision in his handling of a French and a Petrov Defence suggested that he was now playing the match he wanted. If anything, as Fischer moodily admitted, Petrosian could have forced another win in Game Three. The sixth, on 17 and 18 October, may have been the most important of Fischer's whole career. Playing White, Petrosian opened with N–KB3 and launched what is known as a Nimzovich attack. Almost from the word go, Fischer initiated counter-play on the queen side. By the nineteenth move, Black had command of the centre. Now on the defensive, Petrosian adopted a passive but very tough pawn formation indentical with that which had yielded him his clinching point over Korchnoi. Fischer's centre looked overextended, and at the adjournment a clutch of analysts predicted victory, if not a certain draw, for White. The next day, however, Fischer's greatness came into its own: he created an ideal berth for his bishop, set up a mating threat with his rook on move fifty-nine, and forced resignation only seven moves thereafter. On 19 October, Petrosian abandoned his customary tactics. He had to attack in order to survive. Fischer, playing White, maintained a delicate poise between development (the novel, finely measured P–QB4 on move eight) and an alert defence. He took twenty minutes of reflection to refute Petrosian's most dangerous manoeuvre; by move fourteen he had forced Petrosian to trade queens and to go over to an awkward defence. Spassky's analysis, published in the June issue of *Soviet Life*, takes up the inevitable story after move twenty-two: 'In exchanging his powerful knight for the bishop, the American grandmaster calculated unerringly that this was the clearest and most economical road to victory. Now all the files are at White's disposal.' The end came on the thirty-fourth move under threat of a mate in four. After which the match was virtually over. A shell-shocked Petrosian lost the two closing games. Fischer's score in the three Candidates' Matches: 6–0, 6–0, $6\frac{1}{2}$–$2\frac{1}{2}$.

No bare statement conveys the magnitude and impact of these results. At the senior level, chess masters are ranked only fractional points apart. A one-point margin in a tournament or a match is regarded as perfectly satisfactory. It can be argued that Taimanov ought never to have been in the ballpark. But Petrosian had just been, and Larsen might at any time become, world champion. A close win over either, let alone both, would have constituted a major accomplishment. Instead, Fischer sowed devastation. Larsen left Denver mentally and physically sledgehammered. 'Petrosian's spirit was completely broken after the sixth game of the match', reports the Russian grandmaster Yuri Averbakh, who had been Petrosian's second. Buenos Aires left the chess world stunned, and from that moment on Fischer assumed mythical dimensions not only among his peers – were there any now? – but throughout the world press, radio, and television. 'No living player – indeed, no player who ever lived – can stand up to the genius from Brooklyn' (Schonberg). Fischer is 'the most individualistic, intransigent, uncommunicative, uncooperative, solitary, self-contained, and independent chess master of all time, the loneliest chess champion in the world. He is also the strongest player in the world. In fact, the strongest player who ever lived' (Larry Evans, grandmaster and Fischer's second in the match against Petrosian).

Are these proclamations of total supremacy true? We simply do not know. It is almost meaningless to compare Fischer with

Morphy, Lasker, Capablanca, or Alekhine except on the precise level of style. The analytical aspects of chess, the memory content required for theoretical mastery have expanded so enormously since the nineteen-thirties that it makes little sense to ask whether Fischer could have beaten Capablanca in, say, 1928, or whether Alekhine at the crest of his vertiginous form would not have refuted even the sharpest of Fischer's lines, or whether Lasker would not have spotted and exploited certain minute gaps in Fischer's equipment, particularly in complex openings. Unquestionably, however, the Larsen and Petrosian matches of 1971 had secured Fischer's standing among the immortals of the game. They had, furthermore, thrown into relief one of the most fascinating, problematic qualities of his success. Fischer does not merely outplay opponents; he leaves them bodily and mentally gutted. 'I myself have met Fischer many times over the board', records Keres, 'and know how difficult it is to meet an opponent who is always fighting, seeking winning lines in the most dull position, and forcing you to be extremely careful at every moment of the game.' Most players feel that there is more to it than that. They would concur with Averbakh: 'There is some strange magnetic influence in Bobby that spiritually wrecks his opponents.' He seems to possess a destructive edge from the moment he strides into the hall (though 'strides' may be the wrong word to define his loosely menacing, rather slurring gait). Fischer's brutal mannerisms, the unnerving monomania of an acute brain with an I.Q. which unsubstantiated but persistant rumour puts in the 180's, concentrating on a single target, the deliberately humiliating, destructive lunge of the man's mind and hand across the board are probably unmatched in even the ferocious annals of chess. Fischer himself speaks of the exultant instant in which he feels 'the ego of the other player crumbling'. Reportedly, he plays through solitary games in the anonymous hotel rooms that have been his unnoticed home, yelling 'Crunch!' 'Chop!' 'Smash!' 'Zap!' and 'Crash!' as his supple fingers dart across his pocket set. When other men play alone, one half of them loses; I imagine that Bobby Fischer, by some act of schizophrenic magic, has always won.

Whatever the intricate psychological forces at his command, Fischer had since March, 1970, exhibited a degree of demonic violence and technical assurance that reduced his adversaries to numb groping. 'The master will study for hours and perhaps make the right move', says Evans. 'But Fischer will toss out the moves, on his fingertips, and they will be the unerringly correct ones.' The Larsen, the Petrosian, the Spassky who faced Fischer were not the same men who had beaten him or drawn with him on previous occasions; they were not even their customary selves. Fischer agrees, with a bored shrug, that 'people have been playing me below strength for fifteen years'. He left Buenos Aires in a blaze of triumph and worldwide publicity – but also reluctant to fly, lest the Commies sabotage his plane. Now, suddenly, the astronomic monetary demands he had been making for some time seemed plausible. His contempt for Soviet masters seemed justified. His choleric dictum that he had in fact been world champion all along rang true. He had become, according to Schonberg, 'an American folk hero, like John Wayne or Joe Namath'. He has pulled ahead of Van Cliburn on the Soviet charts of the most admired foreigners. In eastern Siberia, a state farm named its prize heifer Bobby. No one bridled at the arrogant discourtesy of the word order when Fischer announced that there was now nothing left for him to do except settle, in straight games, 'this little thing between me and Spassky'.

Notoriously, 'this little thing' came within a hairbreadth of never taking place. Had it not been for the incredible restraint of Spassky and the Russian camp, for the cool nerve of the referee, the German grandmaster Lothar Schmid, and for the desperate patience of the Icelandic Chess Federation, the match would not have begun or would, at best, have broken off in its early stages. Bobby Fischer's personal and public behaviour immediately prior to and during the match fluctuated around extremes of disagreeableness and egomania that the laws of libel make it difficult to report. *Time*'s vignette (31 July) of the challenger's whereabouts when he was supposed to be in the hall playing the second game is presumably accurate: 'Bobby, stripped to his underwear, sits playing chess in his hotel room, the door bolted, the telephone pulled from the wall'. But it hardly tells the story of incredible rudeness, infantile greed, and perfect indifference to the work, hopes, and dignity of other human beings. It all began, of course, with Fischer's failure to appear in Reykjavik on or before 2 July, the agreed-upon date of the opening game. Ducking in and out of Kennedy Airport like Garbo pursued, the self-declared 'champion of the Free World' cancelled booking after booking. He demanded fees high above those previously fixed, which Iceland had raised after intensive efforts. When Fischer condescended to fly, two other passengers having been knocked off a fully booked plane, it was only because a London investment banker, James D. Slater, put up fifty thousand pounds of his own money to boost the purse to two hundred and fifty thousand dollars. After rescuing the whole event by ruling that Fischer could turn up a week late and behave like a hooligan, Dr. Max Euwe, publicly humiliated by Fischer's continued vagaries and by Russian criticism, went home in disgust. One of Fischer's lawyers – they form a vital part of his somewhat grotesque, partly sycophantic, partly truculent retinue – extracted from Fischer an abject apology to Spassky: 'Please accept my sincerest apology for my disrespectful behaviour in not attending the opening ceremony. I simply became carried away by my petty dispute over money with the Icelandic chess organizers. I have offended you and your country, where chess has a prestigious position.' In fact, trouble was just beginning. Having lost the first game, Fischer turned wild. When Reykjavik was first mooted, he had been contemptuous of so obscure a locale, away from the reach of his 'millions of fans'. Only complete, unprecedented television coverage of every zapping move could compensate for such drab remoteness. Glad to defray some of their crushing financial commitment, the Icelanders negotiated a contract for filming (rumoured to be worth sixty-seven thousand five hundred dollars) with Chester Fox and Company, which was to connect with the American Broadcasting Company and other customers throughout the world. Now Fischer declared that he found Mr. Fox totally intolerable and that the cameras bothered him. The frenzies and wrangles that followed are hardly credible. To have seen Fox's lawyer brandishing a vast, wet cigar at the profoundly courteous and restrained Icelandic Minister of Justice and prophesying mayhem if 'those cameras aren't put back where the contract stipulates' is to have been taught a memorable lesson in the tone of big-power politics. In part, no doubt, the fault lay with the world chess organization. It turned out that the match was being played under two sets of clumsily-worded rules, the FIDE code and an *ad hoc* agreement negotiated in Amsterdam between the Russians and Colonel Edmund B. Edmondson, representing Fischer and the United States Chess Federation. Fischer had orally O.K.'d the Amsterdam protocol, but he had not signed it. In the interim, moreover, he had had a row with the Colonel – long a sort of father figure to him – and Fischer now proclaimed that neither the officials of the United States Chess Federation nor any other mortal could bind him to some dim piece of notarized paper. Statement followed on statement, meeting on meeting, regarding the legal force of and possible contradictions among Article 5 (A player forfeits if he does not appear in the hall one hour after his clock is started), Article 12 (A player can protest against forfeiture or anything else if he files his complaint within six hours of the game), and Article 21, an utterly opaque bit of verbiage about cameras and noise. Another attorney arrived to represent Fischer: sleepless but suave, Andrew Davis pontificated on the differences between common law and code law, and suggested that the Soviets could scarcely be expected to grasp the high decencies of the Western view of contract. Under fierce pressure, Lothar Schmid stuck to his guns and awarded the second game, for which Fischer had refused to appear, to Spassky (who had quit the poisoned atmosphere and gone fishing). Fischer booked no fewer than three flights out. He consented to play the third game only when Spassky, with extraordinary gentleness, agreed to meet him in a tiny room behind the stage. But the furious wrangle over TV went on. Chester Forte, of A.B.C., took over from the unfortunate Fox and announced, 'I'm waiting for Bobby. Anything he says goes'.

39

What went, after a last savage tantrum by Fischer on 28 July, was the cameras and crews. Very likely suits and countersuits will bore the courts for a long time to come.

This legal circus was only one aspect of the whole of Fischer's behaviour pattern. Though by definition junior to the world champion, and his guest, Fischer came late for the opening game and for almost every game thereafter. Having been offered a choice among eight superb chessboards and sets, Fischer found none acceptable; after the sixth game, however, he suddenly opined that he might, after all, like the sumptuous marble-and-mahogany chess table that Icelandic craftsmen had prepared as a tribute to the contestants. Of thirteen proposed chairs, none were acceptable. At a cost of five hundred and twenty-eight dollars, an exact duplicate of the four-hundred-and-seventy-dollar metal-and-black-leather job in which Fischer had swivelled at Buenos Aires was flown in. Exasperated by the visible inequality of the resulting arrangement, Icelandic chess fans managed to provide Spassky with a comparable chair at the end of July – not that the champion had voiced the slightest complaint. Almost every day brought its new barrage of more or less megalomaniac exigencies from the challenger. Only victory brought any sign of normal good manners. When matters were not going well – for example, after Spassky's blazing win in the eleventh game – Fischer would instantly revert to irascible histrionics, both in the hall and outside. Having seen to some complicated errand for the super-star, one American grandmaster and former friend was heard to mutter in disbelief, 'Bobby's real sick. He stopped chewing the rug and said "Thank you".' The effect of all this on Boris Spassky will continue to be argued by psychologists and historians of chess. The Russian master behaved thoughout with impeccable modesty and scruple. Fischer's tactics, from mid-June on, kept the situation under constant threat of disruption and did much to debase even its finest episodes. Reporting from Iceland on 22 July, the English master player and chess writer Sir Henry Golombek, who had replaced the appalled Max Euwe as senior representative of FIDE, confessed to a sense of total unreality. It looked to him as if Fischer were 'the greatest anarch of all time'. The remark does not seem excessive to anyone who watched Boris Spassky's features go literally grey with disgust and sadness when he quit the table on 13 July after waiting in vain for the challenger to put in an appearance for the second game.

But all these puerilities and cliffhanging squabbles have been reported *ad nauseam* in the world press. The really interesting question remains: Why did Bobby Fischer, who had expressly set the world crown as his supreme target, who had a dozen times spoken of his certainty of victory in the match with Spassky, come within an ace of throwing away the title, its enormous financial rewards, and the golden opportunity to avenge himself on the Soviet evildoers? He must have been perfectly cognizant of the fact that there were a dozen occasions before his delayed arrival in Reykjavik and during the first ten days of play on which the Russians could have walked out and on which the referee and FIDE might have confirmed Spassky's title by default. This would undoubtedly have been the outcome had Fischer actually taken off from the island on 16 July. (He was reportedly on his way to the airfield at Keflavik when he was informed that the third game would, as he had demanded, be played in a small private room.) Was he playing poker with crazy nerve, pushing his demands further and further in the calculated conviction that they would be met? Had he gone money-mad now that profits undreamed of in chess history seemed to lie only inches away? Was he, deep down, afraid of Boris Spassky, whom he had never beaten, but who had defeated him three times? Or was he beginning to lose his grip on reality? Each of these hypotheses was advanced and furiously argued over during the empty, vaguely hysterical days when Fischer was reported on every plane from Kennedy Airport yet did not come. When the first game went to Spassky after a blunder by Fischer and the second was forfeited, amateur psychology ran wild. Sober grandmasters confidently predicted that 'Bobby will not play chess again'. He would vanish into a rancorous twilight only to reappear as a mysterious hustler in an Eastern Utah State Open (First Prize: $25) on some future winter night. It was noised about that he had 'snapped', that the Russian chess psychologist Krogius was being called in. As it happened, Hamlet sauntered back into the play on Sunday afternoon, took the immediate offensive with Black in a Modern Benoni, found a superb eleventh move, and adjourned in a mercilessly won position. Nonetheless, the puzzle remains: What accounts for his destructive and self-destructive conduct?

No one answer will work. First of all, it should be noted that some of Fischer's exactions and compulsive niceties were thoroughly justified. To a chess mind as incredibly fine-tuned as his, the exact size and hue of the squares, the design and size of the pieces are presumably a vital element of instantaneous grasp, of spatial and relational intuition. The spectators at a world-title match should not be heard to rustle candy wrappers (*vide* furious protest after Game Twelve). The whole television arrangement was a blatant gimmick and inappropriate to such a static, non-gestural spectacle as chess. (But who had clamoured for it in the first place, and is there any truth to the gossip that Fischer's rages were provoked less by the imperceptible presence of the lens than by the fact that his demands for a bigger slice of the film rights had been blocked?) Secondly, there is the simplistic rawness of Fischer's politics – his apparent conviction that the Communists were devils out to destroy him. 'The Russians cheat at chess to keep the world title. They have tried by every means to avoid me. They also slandered my name. They are afraid of me. . . . I should have been the world champion ten years ago.' Given this conviction and some sycophantic Red-baiting in his entourage, Fischer came to Reykjavik with what Spassky termed 'a persecution complex'. Fischer postulated from the outset that not only the Soviet delegation but FIDE, the match judges, and the Icelandic chess authorities were in hypocritical league against him. Only by keeping them off balance, by taking the offensive on every minute point of procedure and material circumstance, would he be able to foil their plots.

The money angle is more intricate. (One would like to know what contractual arrangements bound Fischer to *Life*, whose representative was his constant shadow, and at crucial moments around 13 July, his spokesman.) Without question, Fischer had long and properly felt that the financial rewards available to his genius were ludicrously meagre. Why should Muhammad Ali – a parallel often cited in the Fischer camp – get millions even when he lost, while a victorious unique star such as Fischer picked up crumbs? Why should a chess player in America grub anxiously to make a living, while those 'Commie cheaters' kept their chess masters in the lap of luxury and material security? With Fischer on top, things would be otherwise. He was reportedly asking one million dollars from interested publishers for the rights to his own 'book of the match' (a dozen books by lesser lights having already been commissioned). He would require titanic purses for future world-title challenges, whether FIDE liked it or not. Chess would no longer go hungry in the West. Obviously, the money itself mattered to him. But Spassky, who thought long about Fischer's antics, suggested that the actual cash counted for less than the symbolic triumph – indeed, scandal – that these ransom demands implied. By imposing his unheard-of financial terms, Fischer was once more asserting his individuality.

A lot has been and will be written about Bobby Fischer's character. Most of it is trivia, if only because very few observers can claim any real intimacy with him. It is patent that Fischer is a human being for whom chess is not 'like life' but life itself. He exists, says Euwe, 'in a world entirely his own'. If reporters are to be trusted, he is almost illiterate as far as general civilization goes. Asked by a B.B.C. interviewer whether he was expanding his intellectual interests, Fischer pondered for a while and then mentioned that he was now reading *Playboy* regularly. It is said that the Fu Manchu stories are among the very few works of literature he has found rewarding. This may be mildly suggestive in view of their plot structure, which concerns the endeavours of a superbrain to take over the world. Fischer has Tarzan stories read to him when he is bored, and he likes to go bowling. The rest is silence and sixty-four squares of opposite colours with twice sixteen pieces ditto.

The cutting edge, the rapidity, the precision of Fischer's intellect as a chess player, his memory for every aspect of the game are breathtaking. At certain very special levels, his cortex is operating under pressures and with an efficacy that ordinary men and women and, it would appear, most of his competitors cannot sustain. Almost the totality of his cerebral, nervous even bodily resources are compacted to focus, to 'laser in', on a severely delimited area. Presumably the internal disequilibrium, the reductions of response to the rest of reality must be drastic. When aides and plenipotentiaries hammered interminably on Fischer's locked door, pointing out to him that he would throw away the supreme goal and chance of his life if he continued to boycott the match, that millions of chess fans all over the world were turning angrily against him, a genuinely baffled voice was heard asking what all the lather was about. Surely everyone knew that Spassky was no good, that he, Fischer, could whip him at any time or place, and had, in fact, been the true world champion all along. What possible difference would it make whether or not he zapped the poor *patzer* here and now? The links with reality were hair-thin. But they held. Even at their most strident, Fischer's egomanias and erratic flings masked a shrewd prudence, a somnambular instinct for safety and vantage at the brink. The challenger turned back from the airport. He did not break off when the organizers presented him with the ultimatum that all subsequent games must be held in the proper hall. If Fischer's behaviour, moreover, is more constantly outrageous than that of any other living master, and more cynically opportunistic, it is not the most extreme on historical record. I have referred to Morphy's persecution complex and to Alekhine's psychotic moments. Steinitz reportedly announced that he had played God at pawn odds and won – a claim one is disposed to doubt, only because Steinitz's technique was at that stage no longer top-flight. The issue is larger than the individual case. Whatever Fischer's indiosyncrasies, there are abundant impulses to paranoia and unreality in chess iself, in the violence and autistic passion of the game.

44

Like the inner workings of mathematics and of music, these qualities are next to impossible to communicate in words. Vladimir Nabokov comes as near as anyone has: 'Luzhin, preparing an attack for which it was first necessary to explore a maze of variations, where his every step aroused a perilous echo, began a long meditation. He needed, it seemed, to make one last prodigious effort and he would find the secret move leading to victory. Suddenly something occurred outside his being – a scorching pain – and he let out a loud cry, shaking his hand, stung by the flame of a match, which he had lit and forgotten to apply to his cigarette. The pain immediately passed, but in the fiery gap he had seen something unbearably awesome – the full horror of the abysmal depths of chess. He glanced at the chessboard, and his brain wilted from unprecedented weariness. But the chessmen were pitiless; they held and absorbed him. There was horror in this, but in this also was the sole harmony, for what else exists in the world besides chess?' Something of this full horror and harmony of the abysmal depths, of the magic of chess vertigo, can be expressed numerically. The first four moves can lead to seventy thousand different positions. The number of possible ways of playing the first ten moves on each side is such that if every man, woman, and child on the earth played without respite it would require more than two hundred and seventeen billion years to go through them all. The most recent estimate of the number of different games that can be played is of the order of 25×10^{115}, a product fantastically larger than the generally assumed sum of atoms in the universe. This does not mean that identical *positions* will not turn up. Openings will often run the same course, and an end-game problem set by al-Adli in an Arab manuscript of the ninth century came up in actual play in 1945 (Jorgensen-Sorensen). But the odds against a duplication of a major portion of a game are far more than astronomical. In brief, as far as we can look ahead to a future for the species and this galaxy the variety of play in chess remains inexhaustible.

But these vulgar immensities give little inkling of the maelstrom deeps of the game. Even before start of play, the pieces, with their subtle insinuation of near-human malevolence, confront each other across an electric silence. At the first move, that silence seems to shred like stretched silk. Space breaks into weirdly symmetrical halves. The mirror has sudden spikes, it advances to destroy one. Each move enacts the numbing postulate of modern cosmology that there is not a motion in the universe which does not affect and is not affected by every other motion, that all mass and energy interact in a lattice so finespun, so multidimensional that we cannot even conceive of a model. The dynamic dovetailing of the whole game, the unfolding ramifications of its crystalline armature are implosive in the very first move. But every subsequent move initiates a new reality of potential attack, of masked redeployment in a labyrinth of echoes and mirrors, stalked by the teasing presence of all games previously played on the earth but also new and blank as a sudden crevasse. As the game develops and the clock ticks, a dim weight drags at the mind. It lightens momentarily, revealing the hidden logic of the position, the tensed, marvellously interwoven harmonies that underlie, that must ultimately control the opaque violence of the contest. But then it closes in again, and one struggles as in a stifling smog. The bright arcs of relation that weld the pieces into a phalanx, that make one's defence a poison-tipped porcupine shiver into vague filaments. The chords dissolve. The pawn in one's sweating hand withers to mere wood or plastic. A tunnel of inanity yawns, boring and bottomless. As from another world comes the appalling suggestion – not so much a voice as the needling of exhaustion – that this is, after all, 'only a game'. If one entertains that annihilating proposition even for an instant, one is done for. (It seemed to flash across Boris Spassky's drawn features for a fraction of a second before the sixty-ninth move of the thirteenth game.) Normally, the opponent makes his move and in that menacing moment addiction comes again. New lines of force light up in the clearing haze, the hunched intellect straightens up and takes in the sweep of the board, cacophony subsides, and the instruments mesh into unison. Perhaps there is a win to be snatched after all. As one breathes in the first scent of victory – a musky, heady, faintly metallic aura, totally indescribable to a non-player – the skin tautens at one's temples, and one's fingers throb. The poets lie about orgasm. It is a small, chancy business, its particularities immediately effaced even from the most roseate memories, compared to the crescendo of triumph in chess, to the tide of light and release that races over mind and knotted body as the opponent's king, inert in the fatal web one has spun, falls on the board. More often than not, of course, it is one's own king. And, once again, it is almost useless to seek to convey to a non-addict the desolation of defeat. As in no other game, or even mode of combat, defeat at chess tracks the ego to its final lair. Defeat can, by definition, spring solely from one's own error. There is a mode of chess problems called self-mate: it consists of discovering the unique sequence of moves that forces the opponent, whether he will or not, to checkmate one's own king. Mirror is made to kill mirror. Though baroque, this device dramatizes the essentially suicidal, self-destructive meaning of every lost game. The aftermath is abjection, a corrosive humiliation that drags over one whenever the position is recalled and reanalysed. Hours after play has ended, one wakes to find the night buzzing with jeering forms. The right move was so terribly near, so glaring in its urgent obviousness. Every kibitzer and blind tyro in the room must have seen it. Now it claws at one's skull. But no defeat can be repaired. Time makes every howler, every farcical blunder immutable. Better die than sit down again in front of those torturing squares, than feel again, spiralling up one's bent back and damp neck, the sour burn of defeat. But morning comes, and in the first light the pieces wait, magnetic with the treacherous promise of a better day. 'For what else exists in the world besides chess?'

For a chess master, this rhetorical extravagance connotes sober fact. The complexity of the modern game is such that proficiency is a full-time job. A comprehensive, but by no means exhaustive, chess library would now comprise some twenty thousand books and monographs. This figure does not include the incessant stream of chess journals, many of them minutely specialized. Not even Bobby Fischer can have a complete knowledge of all opening lines and defences. Major openings such as the Open or Closed Ruy Lopez, the Benoni, the Sicilian Dragon, the Grünfeld Defence, the English, the Queen's Gambit Accepted or Declined, the King's Gambit, the Giuoco Piano, the Caro-Kann Defence, the King's Indian, the Nimzo-Indian, the Réti, the French Defence, the Danish Gambit, the Pirc Defence, and the Alekhine Defence are the objects of intensive individual study. To master even two or three of these lines of strategy in depth requires constant study and updating. Hardly a month passes without the publication, either on theoretical grounds or as a result of across-the-board play, of some new variation of a well-known line. Only rigorous analysis will reveal whether the innovation is sound or susceptible of decisive refutation. But the expertise of the professional must go far beyond the generally played and documented lines. He must be aware of the Larsen-Santasière Variation of the Sicilian (1. P–K4, P–QB4; 2. P–KB4) and know that the threats to Black seem worse than they are. He must recognize From's Gambit and recall, if at all possible, the consequences to which it led in the game between Kopylov and Renter in the U.S.S.R. Championship, 1950. He cannot afford to ignore the Wilkes-Barre Variation of the Two Knights' Defence, particularly since the present state of knowledge about N–Q5 on the eighth move is incomplete and since Black seems to derive real chances from the ensuing tangle. At some exact place in his mind, he must store the knowledge that Golombek's improvement (O–O on the eleventh move) of the Manhattan Variation has been shown to be weak and that the whole position is scrutinized in depth in Taimanov's monograph, available in Russian and German, *Queen's Gambit to Dutch*. The master's knowledge, moreover, can never be static. Lines of attack and sacrifice, traps long buried in the records of nineteenth-century mayhem can leap back to life. There are barbs still in the Evans Gambit and Hungarian Defence. In Riga, in 1951, the young Spassky found himself suddenly confronted with the very rarely played Ponziani Opening; in 1959, he himself explored what chances lay in the old Albin Counter Gambit (1. P–Q4, P–Q4;

2. P–QB4, P–K4). I have seen the long-neglected Scotch Game, with which Siegbert Tarrasch won a fine victory over Jacques Mieses in their great 1916 match, tie up and finally defeat an international master in simultaneous play against a much weaker opponent. Powerfully used by Spassky in his defeat of Tal in 1965, the unfashionable Marshall Defence against the Ruy Lopez is now again in vogue. At the same time, new lines, new strategic systems are continually emerging. During the past ten years, an opening system devised by the Austrian master Karl Robatsch has entered the repertoire. Fischer's novel, unorthodox knight manoeuvre on the eleventh move of his third game at Reykjavik has already triggered a flurry of discussion and further trial. Chess may be more than fifteen hundred years old, but even in the openings there are large tracts of the unknown.

The same holds true of the end game. Masters of the Soviet school, such as Smyslov and Grigori Levenfish, have devoted a lifetime of close study to rook endings. The contrasting strengths of bishop and knight, of passed pawns as against immediate material superiority in the closing stages of the game are the objects of a vast technical literature. To players such as Botvinnik, Reshevsky, or Petrosian, the end game, with its hair-fine equipoise of forces, its minuscule but decisive modulations of temporal and spatial dominance, is the intellectual, aesthetic summit of chess. Here actual play becomes like – indeed, often overlaps with – the arcane perfection, the vertiginous but entirely pellucid depths of composed chess problems. End-game positions devised by such composers as Rinck are the solo partitas of chess, torques and mazes of flawless logical sequence and constraint, in which pawns can be more massive than rooks, in which four or even six queens stalk each other in impotent territorial fury, in which stalemates and draws are as hard-fought and satisfying as the most thunderous mate. But virtuosity in the end game does not depend only on profound tactical judgment. The tournament player will draw on an ever growing, ever more analytically detailed body of annotated precedent. He must have in orderly mental reach an inventory of previous end games in which analogous positions, analogous combinations of pieces have turned up. Under time pressure, he cannot hope to find optimal strategies across the board but must rely for his tactical choices on a recognition of previously explored lines and configurations. From the middle game onward, the expert player is projecting, by inner vision, the terminal situations he must aim for or avoid. He knows, without even thinking, that bishops of opposite colours lead to a draw, that the side whose king first reaches the central squares has a large advantage, that split pawns are a nagging weakness, that a posture on the enemy's seventh rank is often paralysing, that major pieces ought normally to be behind advancing pawns. He knows in what position a lone king can force a draw against king and pawn. But, above all, he remembers the dénouements of previous master encounters. It is because he knows the outcome of Stein-Lutikov (Moscow, 1966) that Fischer chooses the thirteenth move he does against Stein at Sousse in 1967; it is because he remembers that B–N2 on the following move yielded no advantage whatever in Keres-Gligorić (Zurich, 1959) that he plays P–QN4 instead. Analysing an Alekhine Defence (Velimirović-Gipslis, Havana, 1971), Gligorić bases his evaluation of possible alternatives after White's tenth move on endings reached in games between Juchtman and Braitman (1954), Ghizdavu and Suta (1970), and Nicolau and Cafferty (1971). Old paths to quicksands and dead ends beset the player's every step. It is vital that he not retrace them.

Thus, there is hardly a moment in modern chess openings and during the end game that does not depend on book knowledge and profit formidably by it. The schooled player has a telling edge over any but the most inspired of intuitionists. Nowadays, openings are studied and memorized until deep into the middle game, and new variations are annotated up to the twentieth move. Playing Black, Spassky took only twenty-two moves to defeat Novopashin's Ruy Lopez in the Thirty-first U.S.S.R. Championship (Leningrad, 1963). Immediately after the game, Bondarevsky, Spassky's trainer, revealed that he and his charge had examined the particular version of the Marshall

Gambit that Black had chosen right down to the exact move on which White caved in. Such determining prevision is impossible in the manifold lattice of the middle game. But here also rigorous analysis and remembrance of previous play are the key to tactics. It is unclear how far the chess mind can look ahead and how many possible variants it can compare analytically during actual play. Not even Lasker, one supposes, could have evolved over the board an exact view of the fourteen possible sequences of play, *each a win*, that arose from the quiet eighteenth move of one of his games against Steinitz in St. Petersburg in 1895–96. (It seems to me one of the most convincing moves in chess history.) But he must have seen a good deal. The same is true of the multitudinous ramifications that could follow on Botvinnik's fifty-first move during his famous struggle with Fischer at Varna. Analysis after the fact runs to several pages of notation. But a fair measure of profound, incredibly exact analysis and contrastive evaluation must have taken place on the spot. How does the brain manage this feat? In what ways are the thought processes of a chess master different from the home-grown variety?

I have cited Gerald Abrahams on the chess mind. Psychoanalysts such as Ernest Jones and Reuben Fine have put forward dubious explanations of the wellsprings of the game in terms of Oedipal aggression or latent homosexuality. Spassky's shadow in Reykjavik, Krogius, is the author of monographs titled *Man in Chess* (Saratov, 1967) and *On the Psychology of Chess Creativity* (Moscow, 1969). But we know very little. To me, the central consideration is that in only three human pursuits – mathematics, music, chess – have creative results been achieved before puberty. There are numerous spheres in which very young children can produce brilliant imitative effects, but they are strictly that. The young Picasso exactly mimes the drawing technique and palette of his father. Compositions produced by Mozart and Rossini before adolescence are genuinely inventive. Gauss sees deep into some aspects of prime-number theory and algebraic series by the time he is ten. Capablanca and Reshevsky register superbly original chess combinations before their ninth birthdays. This suggests two types of affinity among music, mathematics, and chess. All three are non-verbal. They seem to depend on the interaction of highly abstract dynamic relations with a very strong emphasis on spatial grouping. The solution of a mathematical problem, the resolution of a musical discord or conclusion of a contrapuntal development, the generation of a winning chess position can be envisaged as regroupings, as releases of tension between energy levels so as to achieve a harmoniously efficient posture or configuration. In each instance, deep tensions relating the core of the central nervous system to highly cerebral uses of rules and codes are forced to maximum pressure, and then released, affording a palpable muscular-nervous sensation of repose. The second type of interrelation among the three fields may be neurophysiological in a more obvious – perhaps even genetic – sense. It seems likely that all three involve enormously powerful but narrowly specialized areas of the cortex. These areas can somehow be triggered into life in a very young child and can develop in isolation from the rest of his psyche. Sexually and socially unformed, very possibly backward in every general respect, the child virtuoso or pre-teen-age chess master draws on formidable but wholly localized synapses in the brain. In some way that we do not understand, these absorb nearly the totality of the individual's intelligence. The entire machine can burn out after its dazzling start; this is classically, the case with many mathematical child geniuses. Or the special skill will grow at the expense of almost every other resource of personality. It springs up, it matures in a singular degree of isolation from those normal mechanisms of creativity we have learned to associate with glandular-sexual ripeness. There is evidence, moreover, that the capacities for highly abstract spatial imagining, for the rapid mental calcula-tion and projective analysis that are needed in mathematics, music, and chess may be inherited. The large Jewish presence in topflight chess, as in modern mathematics or mathematical physics and in the performance (though not in the composition) of music, does not look accidental.

But what are the cerebral processes that enable a great

algebraist or chess master to 'see the right answer', to see the correct arrangement of units or pieces in an instantaneous, precisely intuitive flash (an experience often reported in both activities)? What makes it possible for him to 'jump' the intermediary links, confident that he can go back and fill in the gaps at will? What meshing of memory, visualization, and sequential analysis is implicit? The most interesting attempts at an answer derive from efforts to design programs for chess computers. Pioneering work began in 1950, when Claude Shannon, the begetter of modern information theory, published his paper on 'Programming a Computer for Playing Chess'. Since then, the challenge has been taken up in the Soviet Union, where Botvinnik has been one of the moving forces; by the European Atomic Commission, with the advice of Dr. Euwe; and at several centres in the United States, notably Carnegie-Mellon. The stakes are far from trivial. If chess does involve central, creative mental operations, the ability to generate and formalize such operations via a computer would throw light on the whole subject of human intelligence. As Dr. Euwe says, 'if we could design a successful chess machine, we might be able to penetrate into the innermost of man's intellectual capacities'. On a narrower front, chess could provide some understanding of the problems of translation; it is a highly formalized but significant code that transcends all language barriers.

So far, the engineers have fared badly. On the FIDE rating scale, a point system based on past tournament performance, the new world champion stands near twenty-eight hundred. A clutch of international grandmasters comes immediately behind him in the twenty-six- and twenty-five-hundred range. Expert players rank around the two-thousand mark. The best computer performances so far obtained in play between machine and man are of the order of fifteen hundred. This is a bare hundred points above amateur status. For a long time, it was thought that this meagre showing was simply a question of hardware, of the storage capacity and calculating speed of the relevant computer. The technical difficulties are enormous. The choice of the best move is a matter of looking ahead along a tree of possibilities each of whose branches divides into yet further branches. To look twenty-five moves ahead (the length of a very short game), the machine would have to envisage and compare moves of the order of 1 followed by seventy-five zeros. Operating at a rate of one million moves per second – which is five hundred times faster than any system at present in use – the computer would need 10^{69} seconds to complete its calculation. The soundest current estimates put the age of the solar system at *circa* 10^{18} seconds. But with greater storage – i.e., provided with a precisely organized memory of all previous master games in chess history – and greater speed, the computer could, at least in theory, match and surpass the best of human performances. In short, the problem could be simply one of developing more sophisticated hardware.

Very recent thinking, however, no longer accepts this conclusion. It may well be that the whole trial-and-error scheme on which computer programs for chess have been based is naïve, and inconsistent with the actual proceedings of the brain. The human player does not scan the board in any point-by-point way. He operates by complex leaps of highly selective attention. (This has been shown by studying the eye movements of master players.) He will compare alternative moves not by any single method of parallel visualization and sequential calculation but by essentially intuitive thrusts toward possible structures that are related to analogous positions in previous play. In other words, the interactions between immediate perception and stored knowledge are themselves complex and inventive beyond anything reproducible in computers, with their yes-no logic and essentially static memory banks. Furthermore – and this, I think, is crucial – such key concepts as 'advantage', 'sound sacrifice', and 'simplification by exchange', on which the choice of moves will depend, are far too indeterminate, far too subjective and historically fluid to be rigorously defined and formalized. The idea of 'the one optimal move' is, in all but the most elementary or nearly final positions, a crude simplification. As we have seen, many celebrated positions and decisions in the history of master play remain disputed and unfathomed to this day. The vital parameters of psychological bluff, of time pressure, of positional 'feel', of tactics based on a reading of the opponent's personality largely elude formal notation and judgment. They belong to the unbounded exactitudes of art.

Does this mean that there will never be chess computers of any genuine interest? Teams working at M.I.T. and Edinburgh University think otherwise. They are trying to design programs that simulate those features of 'instant ordering of perception' (*Gestalt*) and 'self-teaching' which occur in the human player. Shown a number of objects on a television screen, one computer programmed at M.I.T. can be 'taught' to improve its descriptions and recognitions by processes of comparison and analogy very like those that are crucial to the human mind. Experiments are now in progress to make electronic memory storage dynamic and relational, as human recollection is. Past experience would be no longer 'stacked', as it were, in mere formal sequence but interwoven in what are called 'semantic nets'. Such nets seem to account for the speed and accuracy with which verbal-visual associations between past and present intervene in our cognition of a new object or situation. Professor Donald Michie, of Edinburgh, argues:

If the knowledge of the chess-master were built into a computer program we would see not master chess, but something very much *stronger*. As with other sectors of machine intelligence, rich rewards await even partial solutions to the representation problem. To capture in a formal descriptive scheme the game's delicate structure – it is here that future progress lies, rather than in nanosecond access times, parallel processing, or mega-mega-bit memories.

Be that as it may, our present understanding of chess genius is sketchy at best. The mnemonic powers involved are clearly vast and nearly *sui generis*. It is said that Fischer has a distinct recall of the seven hundred games he has played in matches and tournaments. The feats of absolute memory performed in simultaneous blindfold play – a form of the art that Soviet authorities condemn as perverse and perhaps damaging to the brain – verge on the incredible. The late-eighteenth-century virtuoso François Philidor astounded his contemporaries by a blindfold exhibition against three adversaries. In 1943, Miguel Najdorf played forty boards blindfold. In 1960, George Koltanowski, of Belgium, won fifty games, drew six, and lost none in a consecutive blindfold display. Questioned as to their methods, blindfold masters tend to reply that they do not memorize individual moves and do not visualize each board as a whole. What they commit to memory, in rapid order, are key positions or the crucial zones of a given board. This, I believe, is a decisive clue. The great chess player does not see squares and pieces as discrete units, nor even as abstract counters. He internalizes a very special sense of 'fields of force', of regions characterized, differentiated by the fact that certain events can or cannot take place in them. What matters, thus, is not the particular square, or even piece, but a cluster of potential actions, a space of and for evolving events. Keres makes a profoundly suggestive comment in his annotations to a game he played at the Tallinn International Tournament in February and March of 1971. With regard to the fourteenth move, he writes, 'The sacrifice in this game lies somewhere between the two main types. It is not quite intuitive, nor is it based entirely on calculation of concrete variations. During the game I had the feeling that something must be happening around Q5'. The feeling that something must be happening around Q5, or any other square or group of squares, is the essential indicator. Like the conductor who keeps in ordered mental grasp the enormous array of notes and tempo markings set out vertically and horizontally on the page of a Wagner or a Mahler score, the chess master experiences and retains relations of motion, 'magnetic fields' of conjunction or constraint that wholly transcend the single unit. In memorizing the positions of thirty-two pieces distributed across sixty-four squares – a feat that expert players accomplish in about five seconds – the chess mind does not photograph rows of single counters. It somehow encodes essential groupings of meaningful force (as we do in scanning a spoken or written text) and commits to memory the articulate sinews beneath the external skin.

But, marvellously profound and possibly central as these cerebral techniques are, their object remains totally trivial. In the furor of this past summer, among the millions of words provoked by the events in Reykjavik, this modest truth has been largely forgotten. Chess may well be the deepest, least exhaustible of pastimes, but it is nothing more. Bobby Fischer's assertion that it is 'everything' is merely necessary monomania. The proposition itself is grotesque. *Pace* Goethe, chess is not 'the touchstone of the intellect' but only a radically sterile form of play. The problems it poses are at the same time very deep and utterly trivial. We have no logical-philosophical rubric for this strange amalgam. It may be that pure mathematics shares this mysterious quality of 'trivial' depth, of a form of mental life ultimately insignificant – though enormously meaningful – and trapped in a world of mirrors. Though most of us would abhor the suggestion, this 'non-significance' may extend even to music, and the common bond between chess, music, and mathematics may, finally, be the absence of language. But these are murky epistemological waters. What needs emphasis is the plain fact that a chess genius is a human being who focuses vast, little-understood mental gifts and labours on an ultimately trivial human enterprise. Almost inevitably, this focus produces pathological symptoms of nervous stress and unreality.

There was, in Iceland, a surfeit of both nervous stress and unreality. Having come late to the match and to the actual game, Fischer proceeded to lose the first round. An absurd twenty-ninth move threw away what was a dull but certain draw. The challenger was visibly nervous and impatient. He had never yet beaten Spassky. It may be that the wretched TV cameras actually disturbed him. He gave the impression of a man who, in some complicated way, was afraid of being afraid and was, possibly subconsciously, throwing away a point lest Spassky take it from him by better play. I have already mentioned the humiliating farce of the 'non-game' on 13 July. Fischer was now two points down, and various pundits foretold his imminent psychological collapse. Game Three followed on Sunday, the sixteenth, in a tiny room behind the stage of the Exhibition Hall. Fischer's genius exploded, in a Modern Benoni. Though Black, he immediately took the offensive, and initiated a new, audacious line on his eleventh move. Spassky played like a man paralyzed. By the adjournment, he was 'shuffling wood'; that is, moving pieces to and fro in impotent repetition. The fact that Fischer could play with such ferocious brilliance under pressure of a forfeit and after the hysterical imbroglios of the previous days seemed to shake Spassky. On the next afternoon, the world champion quickly resigned but demanded that future games be played in the large hall. He showed real strength in the opening phases of Game Four, playing a Sicilian with a prepared variation. Fischer found himself taking forty minutes for his first sixteen moves compared to Spassky's nine minutes. A fine pawn sacrifice gave Spassky what looked like a winning line. Then the champion faltered. He allowed an exchange of queens, after which the game smouldered to a draw.

The period from the twentieth to the twenty-third of July probably decided the match. The fifth game was a crushing win for the challenger. It was all over after Spassky committed a glaring blunder on his twenty-seventh move (Q–K3 would have given him safety). A distinct pattern was emerging. Against Fischer's somewhat slack opening play, Spassky was obtaining a modest but genuine advantage. Then he would miss the winning line, get into time trouble, and crumble under Fischer's brusque counter attack. Fischer had needed only seventy-eight minutes to win; Spassky had taken a hundred and thirty-one to lose. With the score even, Fischer fired off a new volley of demands and made it brutally clear that he was now top dog. The largest crowd yet filled the hall on the afternoon of Sunday the twenty-third. Fischer stalked in seven minutes late and, for the second time in his recorded career, opened with his queen-bishop pawn. He then transposed into a standard Queen's Gambit Declined, which Spassky had faced no fewer than ten times in his title match against Petrosian. Nevertheless, the champion played feebly, meeting Fischer's darting advansce with routine, wholly defensive manoeuvres. Fischer transferred his queen to the king side, doubled his rooks, brought his bishop to a key diagonal, and smashed through with a hammering, beautifully logical rook sacrifice. Applause filled the hall, and Boris Spassky joined in, obviously dazed yet entranced by the cruel magic of Fischer's play. In this sixth game, perhaps more than in any other in the match, Fischer showed the kind of total control one associates with Capablanca. In the years ahead, many masters will try to imitate Fischer's strategy of tying down the opponent's forces on the queen side of the board before suddenly using key lateral files to switch his own assault to the king side.

The seventh game (25–26 July) showed another aspect of Fischer's psychological and technical virtuosity. Spassky leaped to the attack, at last opening with his king pawn. Fischer adopted an exceedingly risky, involved version of the Sicilian Defence. Soon he was in acute trouble, his king driven from shelter, his defensive position almost smashed by a series of powerful pawn sacrifices on Spassky's part. Any other player would, I am certain, have sought desperately to consolidate. Instead, Fischer riposted, thrusting his queen deep into Spassky's seemingly invulnerable territory. He played like a man wholly immune to fear, with an uncanny certitude that counterattack would save him. At the adjournment, Spassky took forty minutes to seal his move. Overnight analysis showed beyond doubt that Spassky had found a draw. Playing well, taking risks, he did not find the right continuation after his tenth move and had not come in for the kill. In the eighth game, on Thursday, 27 July, the world champion went to pieces. He found himself in serious time trouble after taking fifty minutes over his eleventh move. His nineteenth move was a puerile howler. As Spassky walked slowly from the hall, Grandmaster Najdorf commented, 'The man is kaput'. Now the action was outside the hall. Fischer staged a tantrum regarding the presence of TV cameras during the eighth game. He demanded an abject apology from Schmid. Schmid refused, but the cameras vanished for good and all. Spassky, on the other hand, pleaded a head cold, postponed the ninth game, and was seen heading for the tennis court with a bemused mien.

Play resumed on Tuesday 1 August. Fischer used a Semi-Tarrasch defence system against Spassky's queen-pawn opening and tried for originality on his ninth move. Playing as if he were ahead in the series, Spassky merely invited exchanges and quickly accepted Fischer's offer of a draw. With Fischer already two points to the good, passive tactics were folly. On Thursday, Spassky came late. Playing Black, he chose the somewhat slow, devious Breyer Defence against Fischer's Ruy Lopez. The clocks tell the story: after seventeen moves Fischer had used forty-six minutes, Spassky seventy; after twenty-four moves Spassky had taken up a hundred and three minutes to Fischer's sixty-nine. Even with a pawn in hand, Spassky seemed incapable of generating either technical mastery or psychological confidence. The game was adjourned on the fortieth move with White having two rooks and three pawns against rook, bishop, and four pawns for Black. On Friday the fourth, a bare three hundred and fifty spectators turned up. Playing with magnificent precision. Fischer needed only sixteen further moves to force Spassky's resignation.

The score now stood at 6½–3½. But in fact Spassky had won only one game, the first. His second full point derived from the forfeit of Game Two. Fischer had won five. Three had been drawn. Spassky had committed gross blunders in the third, fifth, and eighth games (the last being one of the worst displays of blindness recorded in world-class chess). He had failed to press home marked advantages in position or material during the seventh and tenth games. He was in almost perpetual time difficulty, whereas Fischer was playing with rapid ease. To all intents and purposes, the issue had been decided.

And yet the eleventh encounter, on 6 August, gave a glimpse of what might have been. Fischer arrived in a new maroon suit and followed by a personal bodyguard. He played the same Poisoned Pawn Variation of the Najdorf Sicilian that had got him into some difficulty in Game Seven – as if to prove that his earlier instincts had, after all, been right. But this time Spassky had prepared a new manoeuvre. In a sequence of knight moves reminiscent of Petrosian, he trapped Fischer's queen. Fischer could have resigned immediately. He fought on until Spassky had literally wiped him off the board, and, characteristically, waited for the champion to walk away from the table before notifying the referee that he was giving up. Appropriately, the lifetime score between the two men, if one disregards the forfeited second game, stood at five wins each and five draws after this curious game.

Despite a new purple suit, Fischer seemed badly out of tune when he arrived to play the twelfth game. Spassky, in contrast, exhibited a new poise. He took only eleven minutes over his fourteen opening moves; Fischer consumed forty-nine. By the nineteenth move, Fischer had exceeded an hour, whereas Spassky had required only thirty-seven minutes. But the game soon took on an air of deadened balance. Though both players created open files, these seemed to lead nowhere. At the adjournment it looked a certain draw. On 9 August the challenger forced a trade of queens and secured a draw with bishops of opposite colours. That night, Reykjavik hummed with rumours that Spassky had found his form, that acid criticism from Russia had put him in a fighting mood. Fischer looked a trifle worn.

But not for long. In the thirteenth game, using the unfashionable Alekhine Defence against P–K4, Fischer soon took the initiative. Adjournment on the forty-second move saw Fischer a passed pawn to the good and Spassky in a badly tangled defensive bind. The struggle resumed on Friday the eleventh. Fischer arrived twenty-four minutes late and took thirty-six minutes to ponder his sixty-second move. The advance of the king to B3 initiated a subtle, deeply calculated plan of attack. But Spassky continued to defend precisely. He was, observed Larry Evans, 'playing like a genius'. On his sixty-ninth move, the champion blundered fatally: R–B3 ch should have given him at least a draw; instead, he played R–Q1 ch. Visibly exhausted – he had analysed all night and not even gone to the airport to meet his wife, Larissa, who was coming in from Moscow – Spassky suddenly saw his position crumbling. Fischer hovered over him, utterly dominant, impatient to begin his

Sabbath. The game had taken on a cruel physical edge, with Fischer having a stranglehold. On the seventy-fifth move, after two hundred and ninety minutes of play, Spassky resigned. As Fischer scudded out of the light, Spassky sat for a few moments staring at the board. The hall was silent. This thirteenth game was in fact the decider. Not only had Fischer played with magnificent technical resource, turning a passive defence into attack, but Spassky had quite literally caved in under the strain. His concentration had ebbed at key points. I have no doubt that he left the stage on that Friday afternoon knowing he was no longer world champion. But this knowledge was to have liberating consequences.

For the second time, Spassky exercised his right of postponement. Fischer had the nerve to complain about the 'inadequacy' of the medical testimonial submitted by Spassky. He was now, in effect, world champion, and when one of Fischer's lawyers flew in from New York 'with stupendous film offers for Bobby', the new monarch hardly took note. He was in a vengeful mood. Candy wrappers had been heard to rustle in the hall. The front seven rows of spectators were too near. Various satraps were dispatched to threaten Lothar Schmid. Conditions were intolerable. So, at least, the fourteenth game seemed to suggest. It was the poorest of the match. Playing White, Fischer bungled on the twenty-first move and lost a vital pawn. Outside the hall, Spassky's seconds, Geller and Krogius, could hardly contain themselves for joy. Their man now had an almost assured win. Six moves later, Spassky fell into a trap even a *patzer* ought to have seen, and gave the pawn back. Geller's face was a study. The affair wormed its way to a turgid draw on move forty.

The real battle had once again shifted to the arena of farcical legalism and financial bullying. Fischer's camp bombarded Schmid with rude letters alleging that the crowd – now back at a respectable fifteen hundred – had been too noisy. Fischer demanded that $46,875, half the loser's guaranteed share, be deposited for him at the United States Embassy in Reykjavik. The Icelandic authorities grimly refused. First the challenger must sign ten presentation chessboards that were to be auctioned in New York in an attempt to recoup some of the losses caused by the collapse of the TV contract. Meanwhile, Mr. Fox announced in New York that he was filing suit for one and three-quarters million dollars and would seek to freeze every cent of Fischer's purse and profits unless television coverage was resumed. (Since then, a second suit has been filed for three and a half million dollars.) 16 August was a degrading day, rife with legal jargon; the smell of money was more cloying than that of fish.

The next six games were draws. But they produced much of the finest chess in the match. Fischer's tactics were obvious: he saw no profit in taking undue risks when every half point brought him inevitably nearer to the world title. Spassky, on the other hand, played with new concentration and real technical finesse. He knew that the world championship, about which he had long felt ambivalent, had slipped from him. Paradoxically, this knowledge seemed to restore his nerve and his pleasure in the game. In the complex fifteenth game, it was Spassky who innovated, on his twelfth move, with Q–N3, and Fischer who blundered, by giving check prematurely. Fischer saved the half point only by forcing perpetual check on the next afternoon.

The hall was packed for the sixteenth game, on 20 August. Fischer played the Exchange Variation of the Ruy Lopez, and a perfectly obvious drawing position was reached by the thirty-fifth move. But the game continued with monotonous tenacity. It went to sixty moves, and Spassky appeared to be saying that Fischer would henceforth have to fight every inch of the way. The seventeenth game was rather weak, and ended in a curious imbroglio. Spassky seemed to have a definite edge at adjournment. On the next day, after only five more moves, Fischer claimed a draw by repetition of position. The referee concurred, and Spassky was left staring at the board. Subsequently, it emerged that the position had not been repeated three times, though Fischer could, it seems, have forced the third repetition. Whether or not this muddle was the cause, the Russians suffered a bout of lunacy. Claiming that Spassky's losses of concentration throughout the match, and particularly on that day, might be the result of secret chemical and electronic devices, they demanded a complete scientific dissection of the playing area. With utter solemnity, chemical engineers and electricians proceed to dismantle Fischer's notorious chair and all the electronic equipment on the stage. Exhaustive scrutiny turned up two dead flies in a lighting fixture. One of Spassky's lieutenants departed for home, reportedly taking the insects to a laboratory for further analysis.

Two exciting games followed. The eighteenth was one of the most tense in the contest. Both players took a hundred minutes over their first twenty-five moves. Playing a Sicilian, Spassky counterattacked strongly on the queen side. Fischer fought off his challenge and may have missed two winning chances. When the battle was adjourned, on the forty-second move, Fischer was revealing obvious symptoms of tiredness. The game ended on the next day by repetition of position. Though only forty moves long, the nineteenth game was very nearly the handsomest in the entire series. Fischer, miraculously, came on time, and he played the same Alekhine Defence he had chosen in the brilliant thirteenth. Spassky produced a fine sacrificial idea, which Fischer refuted after a tremendous struggle. Here was chess of classical fineness between players of equal strength. The resulting draw seems to have left both men very weary, and anxious to terminate the proceedings. The audience on Tuesday, 29 August, was sparse. Spassky, after arriving late, chose the Sicilian against a Richter-Rauzer Attack, and the first ten moves were almost identical with those in the eighteenth game. At the adjournment, Spassky's control of greater space appeared to give him winning chances. But overnight analysis demonstrated that a draw was unavoidable. It ensured on the next day again after a claim based on repetition of position. Fischer was now one point short of supremacy.

The twenty-first game was a sharp duel. Once more, Fischer played a Sicilian. An early exchange of queens should have produced a routine draw, but an oversight by Fischer on move seventeen allowed Spassky to achieve a strong, possibly winning position. Then, on his thirtieth move, the man who for the last time in this match was playing as official world champion blundered. By moving his pawn to KN4, he allowed Fischer to achieve a fatal breakthrough on the king-rook file. Spassky played the last ten moves before adjournment in a kind of mental fog. One last time, his powers of total attention had sagged. Pondering the position, many experts, including Dr. Euwe, thought that White could still find a drawing line. But Spassky was clearly bone-tired. Neither he nor Fischer saw any benefit in prolonging a struggle whose closing rounds had been so very nearly even. Spassky knew that he could not overtake Fischer's lead. He telephoned his resignation to Lothar Schmid at 12.50 p.m. on Friday 1 September. Having obtained a written confirmation, Fischer came on to the stage of the Exhibition Hall at 2.47 p.m. The referee informed an audience of some twenty-five hundred Icelanders, weary journalists, and visiting grandmasters that Robert J. Fischer, of the United States, had won the match and the world championship by a score of $12\frac{1}{2}$–$8\frac{1}{2}$. Applause erupted. Fischer gave an oblique, almost startled glance at the spectators and left quickly. Reached at his hotel, Spassky said, 'There's a new champion. Now I must take a walk and get some fresh air'. He proceeded to do so.

As the lights went down, the pieces were still on the board. The pawn that had given Fischer the world crown stood on R4.

The rest was anticlimax. Fischer arrived almost an hour late at the award ceremony on Sunday, 3 September. He asked Euwe whether he had the money. Then he withdrew to a corner and the buzzing homage of his private phalanx. After a time, Boris Spassky walked over to greet him. Soon both men were analysing and making rapid moves on a pocket chess set. For the first time in almost two months of ferocious intimacy, they spoke to each other. Spassky was smiling.

A number of questions remain. Despite awesome staff work, Spassky's theoretic preparation for the match seems to have been bizarrely inadequate. It was Fischer, the loner, who had completely mastered every line in his opponent's repertoire. It was he who came up with the new ideas and lesser-known variations (the Alekhine, the Pirc-Robatsch, the psychologically startling switch to queen-pawn openings). Fischer's play shone with the kind of theoretic innovations – notably in Games Three, Eight, and Fifteen – that one had expected from the Soviet camp. There is also the enigma of Spassky's numerous howlers. At a conservative estimate, he threw away at least two wins and three draws. By the time he settled down, in Games Fifteen through Twenty, it was too late. And if he committed no more blunders, he did not produce brilliancies, either.

The reasons will be debated for a long time. Fischer's behaviour certainly unsettled Spassky at the start. But it often amused him, and he showed some signs of covert sympathy with a player whose public life was so much more independent and piratical than his own. Spassky's own personality problems, his uneasiness at being champion and representing the Soviet Union in so antagonistic and so important a proceeding weighed heavier than Fischer's antics. There is in Spassky's downfall a distinct element of self-mate. But it remains doubtful whether any other player in the world today could have done even as well as Spassky against Fischer's sheer technical genius and will to victory. The eerie violence and pressure of Fischer's play since his defeat of Petrosian at Belgrade in 1970 are probably without precedent in the records of chess. In a fundamental way, no one could conceive of Fischer's losing now – not even Spassky. That, I feel, is the real sense of this match.

At many points it was not a superlative series. The third, sixth, tenth, eleventh, thirteenth, and nineteenth games were outstanding. Fischer's coolness under all-out assault in the seventh game was superb. Game Six will ensure as a classic of logic and beauty. But the eighth game, despite an innovation on move ten, and the fourteenth were at the nadir of master chess, and such games as the twelfth and the twentieth were extremely dull. The Lasker-Capablanca and Capablanca-Alekhine world-title matches produced more consistently solid chess. Botvinnik and Smyslov, being better matched, played with fewer errors. But all this may be irrelevant. 'This little thing between me and Spassky' has altered the history and the sociology of chess.

Almost overnight, Fischer has transmuted the Byzantine, amateurish economics of the game into very big money. He could become a chess millionaire. In many ways, Fischer's performance at Reykjavik is the quintessence of the American genius for creating immense public excitement and for corrupting through intensity. His reign as champion is certain to bring drastic changes to the mechanics of world-title play. Already, he is speaking of annual matches in Las Vegas or Dallas at stupendous stakes, and of new rules, under which the first man to obtain six wins would be declared champion. FIDE will have to come to terms with the new king or it will quickly lose its influence. As far as Soviet tactics and chess bureaucracy go, Fischer's regime will be traumatic. And throughout the world the inrush of money and media into a hitherto disinterested art is likely to prove a mixed blessing. To an extraordinary number of human beings, however, the events of the summer communicated a rare sense of abstract intensity, and to that extent chess itself is the winner. For several months, a totally esoteric, essentially trivial endeavour, associated with pimply, myopic youths and vaguely comical old men on park benches, held the world enthralled.

1 September marked both Fischer's victory and the start of the cod war. The air was turning grey at the approach of winter as Icelandic gun-boats slipped out of Reykjavik to challenge British fishing trawlers within a unilaterally declared fifty-mile limit and, if possible, drive them off. The game, which is played on squares that are defined on the charts of trawlermen and coast-guard pilots, is an ugly one. Both the Icelanders and the fishermen of Hull and Grimsby are convinced that their livelihood – their way of life itself – is at issue in the match over those icy waters.